Playful Education

Playful Education provides a guide for you to activate the powers of play to boost your teaching practices and increase your effectiveness as an educator. Based on Virginia Axline and Garry Landreth's play therapy, this book is an operational and practical guide on using play therapy to strengthen your holistic learning development and relationships with students. Chapters offer practical responsive interventions for children with behavioral and academic challenges and preventative practices. You will learn the purpose and goals of implementing play times (i.e., PlayBreaks), with individuals and groups of students, skills necessary to facilitate playtimes, and how to transfer play skills to the larger classroom. Educators will learn the foundations of play therapy and how they can be used to guide play within a classroom setting. Expanding beyond the classroom, this book is loaded with playful activities to enhance child-teacher relationships and integrate play throughout the school.

Dee C. Ray is Regents Professor and Elaine Millikan Mathes Professor in Early Childhood Education in the Counseling Program and Director of the Center for Play Therapy at the University of North Texas. Dr. Ray also co-created and oversees the international certification program for Child-Centered Play Therapy and Child-Parent Relationship Therapy.

T0386352

Other Eye On Education Books

Available from Routledge (www.routledge.com/k-12)

Effective Family Engagement Policies:
A Guide for Early Childhood Administrators
Teresa S. McKay

Alphabetics for Emerging Learners:
Building Strong Reading Foundations in PreK
Heidi Anne E. Mesmer

Universal Design for Learning in the Early Childhood Classroom:
Teaching Children of all Languages, Cultures, and
Abilities, Birth – 8 Years
Pamela Brillante and Karen Nemeth

Relationship-Based Early Childhood Professional Development:
Leading and Learning for Equity
Marilyn Chu and Kimberly Sopher-Dunn

The Kinderchat Guide to the Classroom
Heidi Echternacht and Amy Murray

The A in STEAM:
Lesson Plans and Activities for Integrating Art, Ages 0–8
Jerilou J Moore and Kerry P Holmes

Playful Education

Using Play Therapy Strategies to Elevate Your Classroom

Dee C. Ray

Routledge
Taylor & Francis Group

NEW YORK AND LONDON

Designed cover image: © Getty Images

First published 2023
by Routledge
605 Third Avenue, New York, NY 10158

and by Routledge
4 Park Square, Milton Park, Abingdon, Oxon, OX14 4RN

Routledge is an imprint of the Taylor & Francis Group, an informa business

Library of Congress Cataloging-in-Publication Data
Names: Ray, Dee C, author.
Title: Playful education: using play therapy strategies to elevate your classroom / Dee C Ray.
Description: New York, NY: Routledge, 2023. | Includes bibliographical references.
Identifiers: LCCN 2022025855 (print) | LCCN 2022025856 (ebook) | ISBN 9781032259147 (hardback) | ISBN 9781032254128 (paperback) | ISBN 9781003285618 (ebook)
Subjects: LCSH: Play—Psychological aspects. | Play therapy. | Early childhood education. | Teacher effectiveness. | Creative activities and seat work.
Classification: LCC LB1139.35.P55 R39 2023 (print) | LCC LB1139.35.P55 (ebook) | DDC 372.21—dc23/eng/20220810
LC record available at https://lccn.loc.gov/2022025855
LC ebook record available at https://lccn.loc.gov/2022025856

ISBN: 9781032259147 (hbk)
ISBN: 9781032254128 (pbk)
ISBN: 9781003285618 (ebk)

DOI: 10.4324/9781003285618

Typeset in Palatino
by codeMantra

Dedication

This book is dedicated to Ms. Hill,
the teacher who brought play and relationship to my education
And to my always and forever support team, Russ, Elijah, & Noah

Contents

The Child, The Teacher, and Play: An Introduction

Most teachers entered the field of teaching because of a love for children and love of learning. I still remember my first teaching experience and thrill of finally getting to do what I had wanted to do since I was 7 years old. I had wanted to be just like my first grade teacher, Mrs. Hill. Mrs. Hill was a tall thin lady who wore purple and always had the brightest smile. I remember being absolutely in love with her. I thought she was the most beautiful, nicest person I had ever known in my short life. Mrs. Hill was actually my Kindergarten and first grade teacher because she was assigned to our class for 2 years. When I walked to school each day, I looked for flowers to pick for her and gifts from nature to bring to her. She was always so grateful for my gifts which were often weeds that I believed to be flowers, but she would exclaim, "I love them. Thank you so much." And Mrs. Hill was always playful. She would laugh and joke with us. She would play ball with us at recess and run around the playground. She would draw with us and she would listen to our pretend stories as if they were real and interesting. I do not remember anything related to school curriculum from that time, only the fun, play, and feeling a great sense of belonging. I loved going to school those first 2 years and I credit Mrs. Hill with my love and commitment for school and for learning, as well as my deep affinity for the color purple.

My second grade experience could not have been more different. My teacher was unhappy and, even at my young age, I can remember thinking about how unhappy she was. She yelled at us *a lot*. She was angry *a lot*. She never played with us. The first, and only, day I brought her my flowers, she looked at them and then in an annoyed voice said, "These are weeds."

DOI: 10.4324/9781003285618-1

She then immediately threw them in the trash can as I watched. That image will forever be burned in my mind. Striving to be the exemplary student, I managed to stay out of her focus as much as possible. One day, our class was transitioning from PE back to class. We were not standing in line like we should. Ms. Smith (not her real name) began to yell at us with many criticisms, "You're not following the rules. What is wrong with you? Y'all need to learn to do what you're told. What makes you so bad? You are brats." No exaggeration, she literally yelled all of those things at us. When we got back into the classroom, Ms. Smith proceeded to criticize and then asked, "Why are you so good for Ms. Jones (the PE teacher) and so bad for me?" Being a very pleasing and sensitive 7-year-old, I believed she was asking the question sincerely and I wanted to help her understand so she would feel better. And being a naïve 7-year-old, I quickly raised my hand. When she called on me, I said with all the sincerity in the world (I really was trying to help), "Maybe some kids don't like you." Needless to say, that was my first trip to the principal's office. My father was called and had to meet with the principal about my sassiness. I tried to explain, "I like Ms. Smith but some of the other kids don't. I think if she would be nicer, they would like her." I was so confused about how my desire to help was making things worse. And because of this interaction, Ms. Smith never forgave me (even after I drew her an apology picture). I won't go into further details but her attention turned to me and my second grade year was the worst school year of my entire education. I am not a person who has clear memories of much of my childhood but I can remember many moments from that year in vivid detail. Even in fourth grade, I would find excuses to never go down the second grade hallway for fear of running into her.

Within a span of 3 years of my early education, I had one of the best school relationships of my life and one of the worst. What I took from those experiences is that I love learning and that Mrs. Hill was a teacher who really understood me, including my childhood imagination and need for play. What I also understood was that teachers can be scary, I should be quiet, and I cannot trust what I feel or say. Although I continued to excel academically and loved the work of school, I maintained a fairly shy demeanor in school from that point forward. It was the relationships with my teachers that shaped my view, expression, and self-concept in school. It did not matter how many A's I made, they would never make up for feeling inadequate, bad, and misunderstood by Ms. Smith.

And now back to the beginning of this chapter, it became my greatest wish to provide a positive experience for children in school, to be their Mrs. Hill. I studied to be a secondary-level teacher because I was still avoiding those elementary school wounds. When I entered my student teaching experience, I performed competently but I kept getting sidetracked with my interactions with students. I wanted to hear their stories, their feelings, their thoughts. I wanted to know how each individual student approached learning and then I wanted to figure out a way to reach each of them. I became frustrated with not being able to spend time with each of them individually and it soon became clear that I was probably better suited for counseling, rather than teaching. But I never gave up on the dream of building student-teacher relationships that work and contribute to both the teacher and student individually. I have spent 29 years working in schools toward this goal and this book represents the culmination of what I have learned and what has been successful.

Student-Teacher Relationships

The relationship between student and teacher is a primary factor across student achievement, behavior, self-concept, school engagement, and even peer relationships. Hamre and Pianta (2001) revealed that negativity in the teacher-child relationship, as early as kindergarten, predicted problematic academic and behavioral outcomes into middle school. More recently, Gülay Ogelman (2021) found that 5–6 year olds with higher levels of student-teacher relationship closeness also had higher levels of peer acceptance. Behaviorally, more conflict in the student-teacher relationship is associated with increased childhood behavioral problems (Acar et al., 2018; Collins et al., 2017; Hughes et al., 1999; Skalicka et al., 2015).

Student-teacher relationships are highly correlated with a myriad of academic outcomes. Pakarinen et al. (2021) reported that Kindergarten students who were reported by teachers to have more student-teacher conflict also demonstrated lesser interest and skill in literacy and math. Olsen and Huang (2021) found that students with closer student-teacher relationships achieved higher math scores, especially students from lower social-economic backgrounds. When assessing students in ninth grade, students with closer student-teacher relationships in Kindergarten to sixth grade had higher grades, higher enrollment in higher level science courses, higher educational expectations of themselves, greater math and English self-concepts, stronger social skills, and fewer risky behaviors. Valiente et al. (2019) found that boys benefitted specifically in reading when they moved into closer, more positive relationships with teachers from Kindergarten to second grade. Girls benefitted more specifically in math when starting with a close student-teacher relationship in Kindergarten and they were more likely to maintain stable teacher-student relationships from Kindergarten to second grade. Valiente et al. noted that "… when boys' needs for relatedness are met, they are more likely to participate in learning tasks" (p. 117). Researchers have also found that teacher-student relationships are impacted by racial bias and African-American children were found to be at risk for increased teacher-student conflict throughout the elementary school years (Spilt & Hughes, 2015). Spilt and Hughes suggested due to systemic racism, African-American children may benefit even more than their White peers from positive student-teacher relationships and therefore, more training with teachers is needed to provide these relationships.

From Kindergarten to sixth grade, students demonstrate a consistent decrease in student-teacher closeness and an increase in conflict (Ansari et al., 2020; O'Connor, 2010). Ansari et al. (2020) suggested that building elementary school teachers' relationship attitudes and skills is likely to lead to greater personal and academic outcomes for students. In reviewing decades of research on student-teacher relationships, Sabol and Pianta (2012) concluded that the implementation of school, classroom, and individual practices focused on student-teacher relationships would lead to promoting positive outcomes for children and teachers, especially at-risk children. Experts agree that the primary implication of the research on student-teacher relationships is that elementary school teachers benefit from education on the importance of forming close and low-conflict relationships with students and ways to accomplish these goals (Valiente et al., 2019).

A wide body of research supports the cyclical nature of the student-teacher relationship in which interactions shape ongoing interactions, whereby teacher affects student affects teacher affects student and so on. Both student and teacher contribute to the relationship through beliefs and expectations about one another, interactions between the two, and individual characteristics they bring to the relationship (Pianta, 1999). For example, students with higher shyness are less likely to have closer relationships with teachers and more anxious students show more conflict and dependency in teacher relationships (Zee & Roorda, 2018), while a teacher's higher sense of self-efficacy has been shown to contribute to closer student-teacher relationships (O'Connor, 2010). Because adult-child relationships are results of and antecedents for attachment relationships, teachers play a particularly substantial role in children's experiences with attachment figures.

Play in Relationships

At this point, you might be asking yourself, "I picked up a book on play in school so why so much talk about student-teacher relationships?" I found play on my way to figuring out how to build relationships with children, not the other way around. In seeking how to build relationships with children, I participated in endless trainings within the fields of education and counseling. I have learned how to structure children's time, how to design a behavioral plan, how to present information to children in engaging ways, and how to use multiple instructional methods. All of these so-called proven methods fell short in my experience of building relationships with and facilitating change for children. When I was introduced to play therapy, not only did I find an effective mental health intervention, I discovered play as a means to learning and relationship. Play offers a common language between children and adults. Play offers the way to connect and relate to children. Play moves us into the child's world so that we have a better understanding of how they see the world, what needs they have, and what roles adults have in the child's world.

In *The Therapeutic Powers of Play*, Schaefer and Drewes (2014) identified the therapeutic factors involved in children's play and how they can be activated as agents of change. Play facilitates communication through fostering self-expression and providing an environment of learning. Play fosters emotional wellness through allowing children to work through past events or current struggles, eliciting positive emotions, and managing stress. Play enhances social relationships through providing a healthy child-adult relationship, promoting social competence, and strengthening empathy. Finally, play increases personal strengths through increasing creative problem-solving, resiliency, self-esteem, and self-regulation (Schaefer & Drewes, 2014). For the purposes of this book, play exists within and for the purpose of building relationships with children.

Play is the child's language (Axline, 1947; Landreth, 2012). Throughout this book, I will reiterate this statement in alternate ways to remind us that we facilitate play with children in order to speak their language and respect their culture of childhood. In a cross-cultural look at play, Gray (2013; 2019) noted that historically children played all day in hunter-gatherer cultures by acting out activities that were essential to the success of their cultures. Children use play to manage their fears, reduce aggression, innovate and create, promote cooperation, and increase empathy (Gray, 2013; 2019). In early childhood, it is evident that very young children use play more than they use words to learn and communicate. Most adults recognize the play of a 3-year-old as essential to their age and will often engage as the child brings them an empty cup to drink from or stuffed animal to hug. Yet, as children enter school-age, there is an expectation that children will work within the adult world, the verbal world. How many times do parents or teachers say to an upset child, "Use your words"? Yes, children are developing vocabularies and taking on new cognitive tasks but using verbal language to express feelings and thoughts is a struggle for young children.

Imagine this: Luke, a 6-year-old and in first grade, is rushed out of the house in the morning without breakfast, arrives at school late where he is admonished by the teacher, and then proceeds to impulsively push a child who walks a little bit too close to him. The teacher says, "Luke, why did you do that?" Luke is likely to respond with a blank stare, a shrug, or possibly, "He pushed me first." Asking Luke to put together the pattern of stress that he had experienced that morning that led to the push is beyond his cognitive abilities at this point in development. Yet, in recess, an observant teacher might notice that Luke has organized a few children together to play "Beat the runner" wherein each child has to run through four obstacles before another child runs across the playground. Setting up a timed competition allows Luke to express his concern and mastery of time and stress. This is often how play works for children. Sometimes children will use imaginative play to play out scenes related to their lives and sometimes they use other types of play to work out their concerns. In whatever way they use play, they are almost always playing to think through their circumstances, work out their concerns, or communicate their plight. Teachers can expect this use of play frequently for younger elementary ages and forms of various play through older elementary ages. As children gain more complex cognitive abilities, they also gain verbal abilities; yet they will often defer to play as a means to work through emotions and abstract experiences.

Definitions of play abound and include many identified characteristics such as play being fun, novel, purposeless, voluntary, and allow for imagination, among others. When looking across the historical literature, I have surmised that play has four salient features, including (1) activities are free from adult direction; (2) child is actively involved; (3) child experiences a flow with little self-consciousness; and (4) child is released from literal grounding to reality (Ray, 2011). I do not deny that play can also be fun and purposeless; yet, in my experience, those features do not seem to be prerequisites for children to be involved in play. Certainly, play-based activities can be used with children in which children are taught or informed of information through experiential means based on the adult's agenda. However, these types of activities use play as a means to an end, rather than value the play itself. Pellegrini (2019) emphasizes the "means over ends" (p. 167) wherein the value of play is the lack of concern with its usefulness which leads to experimentation. Such experimentation allows children to generate novel ideas and behaviors due to internal motivation and less concern with functionality.

Russ and Lee (2019) discussed the link between imaginative play and divergent thinking. Research has shown that engaging in imaginative play is associated with an increase in children's divergent thinking. Because divergent thinking is the process of generating many ideas, divergent thinking is specifically associated with creativity. The development of divergent think-ing and creativity in play fosters a child's cognitive abilities to problem-solve and initiate new coping skills. A body of research supports the association that pretend play at early ages predicts divergent thinking through adoles-cence (Russ & Lee, 2019). Divergent thinking is the very building block of learning. As children encounter problems, both academic and personal, they are tasked with developing solutions, managing their frustrations, and work-ing with others. Divergent thinking allows for the creativity and emotional regulation necessary for learning at school and in relationships. In play, a child can make anything happen. A child can fly, can be a doctor, or can make a zebra sing. The possibilities are endless. It is within play that a child learns that every situation and every problem can be responded to in many differ-ent ways. In self-directed play within a supportive adult relationship, a child naturally moves toward trying out new ways of thinking and new ways of acting, often going through diverse actions to figure out which ones work to meet the child's needs. The convergence of the benefits of play and the school's goal of education is a solid match, leading to the conclusion that play belongs in schools.

How Does It All Fit Together?

As a play therapist in schools, I value the primacy of human relationships, child development, and play when working with children. Experience has taught me that children learn the most when they are in safe relationships with adults and safe relationships with adults are characterized by accep-tance, trust, and valuing the child's world. When we value the child's world, we value the child's language of play. In this book, I attempt to offer ways in which play can be integrated into schools at the individual, classroom, and school-wide levels for the purpose of nurturing relationships that lead to stronger academic outcomes, reduced student behavioral problems, and joy in teaching and being with children. In the first sentence of this chapter, I stated that most teachers became teachers because of their love for chil-dren and learning. Yet, community and systemic circumstances may begin to chip away at this beneficence. Recently, in a nationwide sample of 15,000 teachers and school personnel, 43% of teachers expressed a desire or plan to quit the profession (McMahon et al., 2022). Teachers are frustrated, children are frustrated, parents are frustrated. Building relationships through play, the language of children, can be a way for teachers to regain their energy and enthusiasm for teaching and working with children. This book serves to present playful relationships as a way to nurture and sustain the joy for teaching.

The purpose of this book is to share the lessons learned from years of play therapy in schools. Play therapy is a mental health intervention that has been implemented in schools from its origin. Because play therapy is designed as a developmentally appropriate intervention for children, it can serve as a preventative practice to help with typical problems of childhood and it serves as an intervention to intercede when children have experienced challenges and struggles beyond their capacities. The practices of play therapy are well-suited to the goals and objectives of schools and can be expanded to involve teachers and all school staff in meeting the developmental needs of children through play and relationship.

I

PLAY THERAPY AND THE ROLE OF PLAY IN THE SCHOOLS

1

What Is Play Therapy and What Does It Have to Do with Schools?

Sara picks up the small elephant. "She's the baby. Everyone hates her because she's dumb. She can't even read."

PLAY THERAPIST: *"No one likes her because she has a hard time reading."*
Sara uses a crying voice for the elephant. "I can't read (in a crying voice) but I like to jump really high (quickly moves the elephant in jumping motion)"
PLAY THERAPIST: *"There are some things that are really hard for her but she can do some things really well"*
SARA: *"Yep!" Sara smiles and continues to have elephant jump.*
PLAY THERAPIST: *"When she jumps, she feels better."*
SARA: *"Yep! And now she's really happy because she's the best jumper."*
PLAY THERAPIST: *"So, when she feels bad, jumping helps her feel happy."*

Play therapy is a developmentally appropriate mental health intervention for children ages 3–10 years old who are experiencing emotional distress or demonstrating behavioral problems. Using the child's natural language of play, the play therapist offers a consistent and safe relationship in which the child can communicate their inner world and real-life experiences. Children intuitively use play symbols (i.e., toys) and scenes to express their thoughts and feelings to work through issues of concern. In play therapy, the therapist facilitates a relationship with the child in which the child feels free to explore their inner experiences and develop new coping skills (Landreth, 2012; Ray, 2011). As children are provided an environment characterized by safety, acceptance, and therefore freedom to explore self, they engage in play to build self-concept, personal responsibility, self-direction, self-acceptance,

DOI: 10.4324/9781003285618-3

decision-making skills, sense of control, self-reliance, coping awareness and skills, internal source of evaluation, and trust (Landreth, 2012).

Virginia Axline (1947) is the founder of Child-Centered Play Therapy, the most widely known and empirically validated play therapy approach. Axline began her career as a teacher. Seeing that children responded to the teacher's relational connection yet seemed to have a distinct language in communicating (i.e., play), Axline pursued methods by which children in the classroom could reach their full potential. When Axline met Carl Rogers (1942), the originator of Person-Centered Therapy, she was immediately intrigued by his approach to therapy which focused on trusting the client to lead therapy sessions where they needed to go and facilitating greater relational depth with the client. In the context of the dominant psychoanalytic theory used up to this point in history and the rise of behaviorism, Rogers offered a novel perspective. Until he met Axline, Rogers had not mastered the use of his approach with children due to the developmental differences between children and adults. He had experimented in working with parents from a person-centered perspective yet had not realized the extent to which person-centered methods could be used with children directly. Being a skilled and successful teacher of young children, Axline made the connections quickly and adapted the person-centered philosophy to individual and group work with children. She developed methods using play as the communication tool with children in order to provide the relationship that appeared so effective in Rogers' work. Although psychoanalytic forms of play therapy had been in use for a few decades prior to Axline (e.g., Freud, 1946; Klein, 1932/1975), she was the first to use a lens of trust and relationship from which to facilitate growth in children. Axline began to study the effectiveness and process of play therapy in the 1940s and continued to do so through the 1960s. In her most famous work, *Dibs: In Search of Self* (Axline, 1964), Axline presented a case of a boy, described as autistic by today's criteria, over the course of a year in play therapy. In this triumphant tale of a child overcoming emotional and contextual barriers, Axline opens the book with observing and meeting Dibs as he defiantly resists and then physically attacks his teacher. Throughout Axline's career, even after leaving the classroom as a teacher, she maintained her involvement in schools and promoted the implementation of play therapy in school settings.

Research on Play Therapy in Schools

Although play therapy is currently accepted as a mental health intervention used in community and private practice counseling settings, the roots of play therapy are still grounded in schools. A considerable amount of research on play therapy effectiveness has been conducted in school settings over the 85 years of play therapy research, leading to a large number of studies that speak to the role of play therapy in facilitating the academic achievement and social-emotional development of children. Many play therapy researchers are inclined to study the process of play therapy in schools because of the diversity of identities, characteristics, environments, and ages found in schools. Over the last three decades, research teams led by play therapy researchers such as Phyllis Post (University of North Carolina-Charlotte), Sue Bratton (University of North Texas), Pedro Blanco and Ryan Holliman (Tarleton State University), Jeff Cochran and Nancy Cochran (University of Tennessee), April Schottelkorb (Boise State University), Karrie Swan (Missouri State University), Yumiko Ogawa (New Jersey City University), Kristi Perryman (University of Arkansas), and myself (University of North Texas) have led research teams that have produced a considerable number of studies contributing to understanding the role of play therapy with children in the school setting. Attachment A presents a compilation of 29 experimental and quasi-experimental research studies conducted in schools since 2000 on play therapy demonstrating its effectiveness on improving academic achievement, reducing anxiety and depression, increasing social-emotional competencies, decreasing aggression and other disruptive behaviors, decreasing post-traumatic stress symptoms, reducing teacher-child relationship stress, and increasing empathy. And unlike most mental health intervention research with children, play therapy studies involve the participation of multicultural samples representing diverse racial and economic communities.

In 2015, my research team conducted a meta-analysis of 23 play therapy experimental studies conducted in schools from 1970 to 2010 which involved exploring the rigor of studies and statistical results for 1106 children (Ray et al., 2015). When pooled, results indicated that play therapy was effective in improving academic achievement, reducing both internalizing and externalizing behavioral problems, improving student self-efficacy, and other issues such as improving social skills and teacher-child relationships. The average number of sessions for these studies was 12 sessions which indicated that play therapy is effective as a short-term intervention in schools. Another interesting finding from this exploration of play therapy studies is that the sample participants comprised a diverse ethnic/racial composition (32% African-American, 37% White, 23% Hispanic, 2% Asian American, and 6% International). The inclusion of diverse participants suggests that effectiveness of play therapy extends to meeting the needs of various cultural communities. Another observation regarding the growth of play therapy in schools is that 23 studies made up the 2015 meta-analysis that spanned over a 40-year period (1970–2010) while 29 studies were conducted in the 20-year span of 2000–2021 denoting a substantial increase in the use and exploration of play therapy in schools.

How Does Play Therapy Work?

In play therapy, there are two main factors at work: the therapeutic relationship and the powers of play. In Chapter 1, I introduced the power of play with children and how children use play to communicate their experiences and perceptions. In this chapter, I am focused on explaining the relationship within play therapy that serves to facilitate therapeutic healing for children. Rogers (1951) introduced his theory of development from which he explained the nature of the person at birth through the development of adaptive or maladaptive ways of being in the world. Understanding Rogers' development theory is crucial to understanding how play therapy works. In person-centered philosophy, a child is born with one basic innate tendency to strive toward actualizing the organism of the individual. This does not mean that the child is born "good" as often misunderstood in person-centered philosophy but it does mean the child is always seen as striving toward a way to improve or maintain as a person, even if engaging in behaviors that seem destructive from the outside. A child is born into a world wherein external events and experiences take place in reality but the child experiences them uniquely from their own perspective. This unique experience of the world becomes the child's reality. Hence, each person has their own reality created from their experiences in the world. A person sees the world from their own reality which may or may not be consistent with others' views of reality. Each person then operates in the world from that perceived reality. Behaviors and emotions flow from that reality and work holistically in tandem to meet each person's needs based on the perceived reality.

So, in order to understand why a child does what they do or feels the way they do, the adult must seek to understand the child's view of reality. What is the child's frame of reference? Through relational experiences (i.e., interactions with others), a child starts to develop a sense of self contextualized in others' evaluations and values. Sometimes these values are taken in through personal experiences while at other times values are adopted from messages of caretakers, other adults, or possibly community systems. A child may form a sense of self that is consistent or inconsistent with these values and engages in behaviors that match this sense of self. For example, a young child may be abused by a parent resulting in the values that I am only acceptable if

(1) I am quiet; (2) I never say what I need; and (3) act tough like things don't hurt me. This child then will act in a manner consistent with these beliefs about the self. These values are called "conditions of worth" (Rogers, 1951), the expectations that must be met in order to be accepted by others and by which a child judges their own personal worth. As the self-concept is constructed, new interactions will be experienced through the formed self that is made up of these values. Therefore, the child who has formed a self based on the conditions in the above example will filter all interactions through this self-structure. If a teacher asks this child to share what they want to do during recess or what help they need in math, the child is likely to not respond at all or that they do not desire or need anything. Even if the teacher is sincerely caring about wanting to meet the child's needs, this interaction is inconsistent with the child's internalized sense of what makes them acceptable and the child will likely rely on the known behaviors that are consistent with the self-structure. In fact, we often see that when children experience new caring interactions different from what they experienced previously, they will perceive these new experiences as threatening. A threat to the self-structure usually results in even greater rigid behaviors. However, the self-structure is not an impermeable structure. With new continued and consistent interactions, a child is able to form new values that are more enhancing to the organism of the person. If the teacher continues to reach out frequently and consistently, the child may start to take in these experiences as (1) my needs are important and cared about and (2) when I share my needs I can figure out ways to meet them. The caution is that any child who has operated under conditions of worth in the self-structure can only become flexible in modifying their perceptions when no threat is perceived. In other words, a child can only start to see themselves differently when they do not feel forced or coerced into changing. The irony is that people will only change when they feel fully accepted (Rogers, 1961). This understanding of how children develop functional impairment is the foundation of why play therapy works.

In child-centered play therapy, the therapist believes in the child's capacity to lead and move toward self- and other-enhancing behaviors. Within the natural state of the child is the desire to be a better person, thrive in their environment, and enhance the lives of others. Yet, through experiences and messages from others or the world-at-large, the child may have developed conditions of worth that send the message that the child must feel or act in certain ways to be of value. In play therapy, therapists strive to lift those conditions of worth in order for the child to develop a self-structure that is consistent with the innate state of being and will naturally move the child toward positive self-concept and coping skills. The therapist sends messages of acceptance, trust, care, consistency, and safety in order for the child to begin to loosen the self-structure and start to imagine new possibilities of self and worth. The therapeutic relationship is not based on what the therapist *does* to the child but on what the therapist provides for the child in the form of relational attitudes and qualities.

Axline (1947) built upon the philosophy of person-centered counseling when she created the eight principles of the therapeutic relationship in play therapy. In summary, the eight principles are:

1   The therapist develops a warm, friendly relationship with the child as soon as possible.
2   The therapist accepts the child exactly as is, not wishing the child were different in some way.
3   The therapist establishes a feeling of permissiveness in the relationship so that the child can fully express thoughts and feelings.
4   The therapist is attuned to the child's feelings and reflects those back to the child to help gain insight into behavior.
5   The therapist respects the child's ability to solve problems, leaving the responsibility to make choices to the child.
6   The therapist does not direct the child's behavior or conversation. The therapist follows the child.
7   The therapist does not attempt to rush therapy, recognizing the gradual nature of the therapeutic process.
8   The therapist sets only those limits that anchor the child to reality or make the child aware of responsibilities in the relationship (pp. 73–74).

As can be noted in the principles, they are prioritized for importance. Although all principles are essential to the application of play therapy, the first primary principle is building a warm relationship with the child while the eighth principle is the setting of limits. In addressing limits, Axline remarked that limits are set as part of relationship responsibilities. In play therapy, even limits are seen as contributing to the relationship, not as tools for compliance.

Garry Landreth (2012), the leading play therapist, author, and trainer of the last 50 years, expanded Axline's work with his seminal work, *Play Therapy: The Art of the Relationship*, now in its fourth edition. It should be noted that Landreth also began his career as a teacher first, then a school counselor. Landreth transformed the world of play therapy through providing the essential nature of relational qualities necessary for the play therapist and operationalization of the play therapy structure. The four healing messages that the therapist sends to the child are simple yet profound: *I am here, I hear you, I understand, I care* (Landreth, 2012). As the therapist offers full presence to the child, engages in listening to the child's play and verbalizations, understands what the child is sharing, and sends a message of care to the child, the child experiences full acceptance in the play therapy relationship. Landreth identified several objectives of play therapy including that the child will (1) develop a more positive self-concept; (2) assume greater self-responsibility; (3) become more self-directing; (4) become more self-reliant; (5) engage in self-determined decision-making; (6) experience a feeling of control; (7) become sensitive to the process of coping; (8) develop an internal sense of self-evaluation; and (9) become more trusting of self. The objectives of play therapy are typically aligned with characteristics that improve academic functioning and serve to augment the school environment.

As I have presented, play therapy research has historically and recently demonstrated the positive effects of play therapy on improved academic achievement. In the series of studies by Blanco, Holliman, and team (see Attachment A), children have consistently shown improvement on standardized testing after participating in play therapy when compared with children who have not received play therapy. It seems logical to question how an intervention that does not involve direct teaching, guided lessons, or any academic curriculum at all can help improve student assessment scores. From the beginning of implementing play therapy in the schools, Axline (1949) addressed this issue by theorizing that play therapy releases a child from emotional barriers limiting the child from performing at full potential in learning environments. As I have conducted pre- and post-academic achievement testing in many play therapy studies, I can attest that children at posttest seem happier, lighter, more willing to engage in the testing process, and confident in their performance.

What Play Therapy Looks Like in Schools

The implementation of play therapy in schools has waxed and waned over the years and across the United States and worldwide. In the 1960s and 1970s, on the heels of Axline's contributions, play therapy grew in popularity and was used in preschools, albeit with limited scope. At this same time, behaviorism rose quickly and ubiquitously throughout schools, becoming embedded in school culture. With the rise of cognitive-behavioral therapy in the 1980s and the continued school allegiance to the principles of behaviorism, play therapy fell out of favor and, presumably, the consciousness of most schools. The 1990s saw a rise in the training, organization, and development of play therapy, resulting in the establishment of the Center for Play Therapy at University of North Texas and the formation of the national Association for Play Therapy

(APT). The Center for Play Therapy became a central hub for play therapy education, and more uniquely, for research in play therapy (cpt.unt.edu). The Association for Play Therapy (a4pt.org) led the advocacy movement for play therapy by increasing educational and networking opportunities while also initiating credentialing of play therapists to ensure quality of care. In 2021, APT reported approximately 5,000 Registered Play Therapists and Registered Play Therapist-Supervisors. Child-centered play therapy became recognized as an evidence-based intervention by national and state organizations in the 2010s. Since 2010, play therapy has become known across the globe for its effectiveness and developmental appropriateness for children.

Play therapy in schools has followed a similar trajectory, yet slower and more meandering. The philosophy of child-centered play therapy is antithetical to the principles of behaviorism which are entrenched in school processes and procedures. Whereas behaviorism is grounded in external reinforcement to move a child toward authority-desired behaviors, play therapy facilitates internal motivation of children to move toward better health and functioning. Although preschools have maintained an interest in implementation of play therapy throughout the years, elementary schools have struggled to see the value of intrinsic motivation tools when behaviorism is seen as the more expedient road to compliance. In many schools, compliance is interpreted as an optimal learning environment. The philosophy of play therapy, which can also be considered a learning theory (Rogers, 1969), holds that children will learn more effectively when they are internally motivated to do so, when they believe that they are worthy of being accomplished or successful, and when they believe that someone cares about them as individuals with their own needs and desires. Another cultural mismatch that undergirds school culture is the expectation that children express themselves through verbal language, either orally or in writing. In play therapy, childhood is recognized as a culture in and of itself whereby the community members speak the language of play and experience. These differences in philosophy have been barriers for the growth of play therapy in schools. However, many school counselors have preserved play therapy in the school setting through advocating for practices and spaces to support their play therapy programs. In the last decade, as schools have seen systemic failures of behaviorism with an increasingly diverse student population, the use of play therapy in schools appears to have grown. In addition to diverse student communities, schools have widened their practices, particularly as the field of education has become more knowledgeable of trauma and adverse childhood experiences (Blodgett & Lanigan, 2018; Jimenez et al., 2016; Zeng et al., 2019). Mental health in the schools is now a focal point for many schools and funding is being provided for additional mental health counselors and social workers. As a result, play therapy appears to be implemented in schools more frequently and more consistently. One indicator of the rise of play therapy in schools is the initiation of the Registered School-Based Play Therapist credential by the APT in 2016.

Play therapy is typically provided for children between 3 and 10 years old to meet their developmental needs. For schools, this means that play therapy programs are targeted toward preschool to fifth grade. Because of the holistic nature of play therapy intervention, any child can benefit from being in play therapy. However, in schools, children who are demonstrating emotional or behavioral problems, disruptive to the school environment, struggling with peers, or not achieving at their academic potential are identified as students who benefit the most from play therapy. As discussed earlier in the chapter, research has shown the effectiveness of play therapy with all of these presenting problems. Children in school play therapy participate in weekly or twice-weekly 30-minute play sessions, although some school-based play therapists are able to extend to the traditional 45-minute session. With consistent provision of play therapy, research has revealed that children will start to demonstrate noticeable change in 10–20 sessions, with substantial changes demonstrable at 20 sessions (Ray et al., 2015). With twice-weekly sessions, this translates to an 8–10 week intervention.

Critical to the effectiveness of play therapy intervention is the education and training of the play therapist. Whether it be the school counselor or mental health professional in the school, effective play therapists have received extensive training and supervision on the provision of play therapy. Play therapy is more than playing games and having fun in a therapy session. Many counselors claim that they are doing "play therapy" because they have games and activity materials in their counseling rooms. Yet, play therapy requires that the play therapist is operating from a consistent theoretical philosophy and has been trained and supervised in evidence-based procedures.

As we come to a close on the explanation of play therapy, you might question, "Am I being asked to be a play therapist?" The answer is an emphatic no. In play therapy, the child is referred for emotional and behavioral problems that have developed through the context of a child's background and environment. The play therapist is responsible for conceptualizing the child's background, worldview, current environment, and the extent of their functionality related to those factors. In play therapy, the play therapist has developed a treatment plan to work with the child and systemic partners, such as parents, caretakers, and teachers, to achieve treatment goals. The play therapist facilitates the relationship and play of the child with the direct goal of fostering new coping skills and new ways of operating in the world.

The current chapter presented definition, change processes, and evidence supporting the use of play therapy in schools in order to provide a foundation for how and why play therapy has much to teach us about how play and relationship can benefit both students and teachers in the school environment. In play therapy, play therapists are attuned to the psychological nature and outcomes of therapy which is required to work with children who have significant mental health issues or barriers to wellness. However, we know that relationships between teachers and children can be healing when children feel close and supported by teachers. Teacher and student relationships predicated on play build systemic support for children who are struggling in school and possibly in life.

2

The Power of Play in the Holistic Learning and Development of Children

The principles of play therapy are based on the powers of play. "Play is not a luxury but rather a crucial dynamic of healthy physical, intellectual, and social-emotional development at all age levels" (Elkind, 2007, p. 4). Play is the parallel precursor to, instigator for, and indicator of growth and development in childhood. In other words, play correlates with children getting ready to learn, the process of learning, and demonstrating what they have learned. Pellegrini (2019) points out that the novel uses of object play conducted by children attracts the attention of other children, thereby creating a learning environment for children to learn from one another. Learning is always taking place when children play. But it may not be the kind of traditional learning with which we are familiar. Children do not enter play with a goal of learning to read or solving a math problem. What happens in play is much more organically driven and holistic. Jonathan, a 6-year-old, sets up a play scene of war with superheroes and villains. He refers to them as good guys and bad guys. The following is an excerpt from Jonathan's narration of his play:

> Jonathan: (very excited) The bad guys build a wall to keep the good guys out. They need all these bricks. (Jonathan grabs 11 bricks. He stacks four rows of three columns but is missing one to make the wall even.) Wait, it's not working. (Jonathan is frustrated by the uneven wall. He stops to count.) I need one more. (He then grabs one more and starts to move the wall into a rectangle shape with right angles. He spends extra time getting the wall corners to come together.) These have to be together so no one can get through. (He now has the wall in a rectangle with no spaces in between connecting points.) There, I did it! (He says proudly).

DOI: 10.4324/9781003285618-4

In this very short play scene (less than 5 minutes), Jonathan has practiced mathematical skills and problem-solving (i.e., addition, possibly multiplication, and geometry), managing his frustration tolerance, and building his self-esteem. In his play, Jonathan naturally moves toward both academic learning and emotional learning without ever realizing these objectives are accomplished. This is the nature of play. Children are spontaneously drawn to learn holistically when driven by their own intrinsic motivations and provided an environment of support for such learning. The end result is the child is further motivated by the fun and success of the endeavor and will continue to engage in seeking challenges in the academic and social-emotional domains.

At a time in history when we see our children suffer from unprecedented levels of anxiety and discouragement, play offers a way in which children can learn with less stress and feel encouraged in their play scenes and accomplishments. Experts have lamented the rise of the inappropriate match of school curriculum and child development (Elkind, 2007; Gray, 2013). The last decade has revealed that children are able to accomplish rigid academic standards at young ages through rote memorization and direct instruction. However, the cost has been high. Our children are more depressed, more anxious, less creative, and less physically active than previous generations. The recent COVID-19 pandemic appears to have exacerbated problems to a boiling point. Preliminary research on the effects of the pandemic indicates that children demonstrated increased externalizing problems, attention problems, and mood symptoms, such as depression and anxiety, when compared to pre-pandemic levels (Spencer et al., 2021). It appears that children who attended virtual schools in comparison with in-person schools exhibit comparatively worse emotional and mental health issues (Verlenden et al., 2021). Additionally, 76% of teachers reported that student behavioral issues were a very or somewhat serious issue for teachers (NEA, 2022). Conducted in the 2020–2021 school year, a survey of 15,000 teachers reported that 33% of teachers had experienced a verbal threat of violence from a student (McMahon et al., 2022). And even more disturbing, physical violence was reported most commonly among elementary school teachers, of whom 26% had been physically assaulted by a student.

Our children are melting down. Teachers are paying the price. Play may not be the only answer but it is surely one of the tools that we know works; yet we do not practice and offer play to our children enough. Decades of research reveals that play is the tool used by children to build their intellect, holistic development, emotional regulation, and social skills. Elkind (2007) identified four types of play that coincide with children's development: mastery, innovative, kinship, and therapeutic. In mastery play, children first use play to explore objects and concepts. Upon understanding of these concepts, children will engage in repetitive play to master the skills they have recently learned. Repetitive play instills a sense of competency and completion for children. Once a child has mastered skills in play, they will want to build on those skills with creativity and expansion. Innovative play unleashes the child's potential to elaborate on what they have learned and develop new, creative ways of thinking and doing. Innovative play can be exemplified through generating jokes and riddles (i.e., building on the mastery of language) or playing out different scenes of an argument between animals (i.e., building on mastery of social interactions). Kinship play is the type of play with which most of us are familiar. Kinship play is peer-to-peer play where children are naturally drawn to one another due to their similar age, size, language, and position in the adult world. In kinship play, children learn how to relate socially with others and practice social skills and empathy. The final category of therapeutic play is play in which children engage in order to deal with and relieve stress. In therapeutic play, a child typically engages in play behaviors that symbolically or concretely mirror stressful events or experiences from their own lives.

It is common to see children practice mastery and innovative play within the context of therapeutic play. For example, a child who has experienced abuse at home may play out an animal scene in which two bigger zebras are fighting and the small zebra runs to hide from them. This is an example of therapeutic play. Once the child has set the scene, the child says that the baby zebra runs to hide to stay safe and plays out all the places the baby zebra can hide (i.e., mastery play). As the play scene develops, which may occur over multiple playtimes, the baby zebra goes to the elephant neighbor's house, or sometimes goes to the park with the monkeys, or sometimes calls someone for help on the phone (i.e., innovative play). Therapeutic play often encompasses all aspects of a child's development including mastery, innovation, regulation, problem-solving, intellect, and feelings. Therapeutic play is used often by children for everyday stressors and can be helpful in solitary or group contexts. However, children who use therapeutic play for more serious traumas or experiences are typically in need of relational support to engage in therapeutic play that results in resolution and regulation.

As children engage in play, they optimize the building blocks of development. Play allows children to take the confusing and overwhelming events of childhood and bring them into a contained environment of a child's own imagination and space. Through toys and materials, the child finds the words to explore and express those things with which the child struggles or is simply curious. And when play is conducted in the presence of another person, the child learns that relationships can support them through struggles and worries. The many variations of play offer the child opportunities to work through spelling or make a friend, practice a science experiment or explore reactions to authority, create a story or walk through how to respond when angry without getting into trouble. These types of play take place every day in the life of the child if we support the play environment and the child's freedom to play.

3

Play and Development

Play begins in infancy and is integral to development across childhood. The most famous of the developmental theorists, Jean Piaget (1896–1980), focused on the typical cognitive development of children expressed through their play behaviors over four stages. The first stage of play in infancy is labeled sensorimotor play and appears as play designed to practice or master basic motor skills (Piaget, 1962). Object play emerges in which infants begin to grasp objects and, in later infancy, explore objects more fully (Hirsh-Pasek & Golinkoff, 2003). Children first appear to play with objects around 12 months of age (Pellegrini, 2019) and increase their object play over the next few years.

In the second year of life, toddlers initiate symbolic play, also referred to as pretend play or imaginative play. Early in this stage of play, children pretend to eat food from a plate or drink from a cup, engaging in play that mimics actions they have seen in real life. As children reach the third year of life, their symbolic play becomes noticeably more complex as they engage in sociodramatic play in which children take on roles and organize play scenes and stories. Sociodramatic play begins slowly at age 3 and increases with more intensity at age 4. The symbolic nature of play accompanies learning language, reading, and problem-solving (Hirsh-Pasek & Golinkoff, 2003).

Following the age of 4, children become more intricate in their play through attention to detail and integration of reality mixed with fantasy. Play in early schooling from 4 to 6 years old involves a particular affinity for and skill in pretend play (Johnson, 2015). This age group is also using gross motor skills and enjoys lots of space to move around in their play. During their play, children learn and create symbols that lead to an explosion of language

DOI: 10.4324/9781003285618-5

acquisition and communication (Elkind, 2007). At this age, children begin to integrate reading and writing spontaneously in their play when in their home environments (Christie & Roskos, 2015). Four- to 6-year-olds play out stories with social and verbal interaction with much energy while 6–8 year olds continue to expand sociodramatic play with more detail and elaboration (Johnson, 2015). Play is associated with development of listening and reading comprehension skills as outcomes of storytelling and narratives that go along with make-believe play behaviors (Roskos, 2019). From 6 to 8 years of age, children are developing their fine motor skills in addition to gross motor skills and start to incorporate more intricacy in their creations (Johnson, 2015).

Elementary school age children begin Kindergarten with high needs for symbolic and social play for expression and problem-solving. Throughout first through third grade, most children continue to prefer symbolic play with both solitary and social opportunities. From third to fifth grade, most children show a preference for social play, with attention to competency and relationship. Play from 8 to 12 years involves skill practice, continued pretend play with integration of literary and personal experiences, games with self-established rules, and constructive play (Bergen & Fromberg, 2015). Throughout play development, children grow in their language abilities and their desire for more social play.

While much of the understanding of play in childhood focuses on cognitive processes, Lev Vygotsky (1896–1934) pursued research in the affective and overall developmental implications of childhood play (Vygotsky, 1966). Claiming that play was the leading source of development in preschool, Vygotsky recognized the role of make-believe play in the holistic development of children. In fact, pretend play is created by children around the age of 3 when the child can no longer make reality fit with desires or tendencies. Through creating imaginary situations, taking on roles, and following self-imposed rules for these roles, children are incited to greater symbolic thinking and imagination (Bodrova & Leong, 2011). Vygotsky is known for three major contributions to the understanding of child play (Hirsh-Pasek & Golinkoff, 2003). Vygotsky proposed the concept of the "zone of proximal development" as a dynamic that occurs in play in which the child acts above their average age, able to reach a higher level of development without the restriction of reality. The second understanding from Vygotsky was that in play, a child is liberated from external constraints through activity in an imaginary situation, thereby allowing a separation of thought and action, contributing to the development of imagination. Finally, Vygotsky suggested that play contributes to the development of self-regulation through the creation of and subordination to self-imposed rules necessary for the play scene (Bodrova & Leong, 2011).

In studying the correlation between imaginative play and child development, Russ et al. (2011) also concentrated on affective and holistic development. They found that play involves affective processes that include expression of positive and negative emotions, expression of personal and experience themes, enjoyment, and integration of emotions cognitively leading to emotional regulation (Russ et al., 2011). Russ et al. (2011) also highlighted the relationship between imaginative play and increased coping skills. Play facilitates problem-solving, flexibility, divergent thinking, alternative coping skills, positive emotion, ability to think about themes, ability to take the perspective of another, and general adjustment.

Brain Development

Historically, our understanding of play has relied on observations of behaviors and interactions, seeking to interpret childhood actions as markers of development. In the last two decades, neuroscience has brought us new information to expand our understanding of development and play based on observations of brain and body functions. Deepening our understanding of brain development furthers our understanding of the role of play in holistic child development. At birth, the developing brain of an infant has about 100 billion neurons with each producing up to 15,000 synapses (Bergen, 2015). Neural cells are also located in the heart and the gut sending messages to the autonomic nervous system (Badenoch, 2018). Through life experiences, neural networks are developed by linking experiences together in the connection of neurons through synapses. Repetition or emotional intensity of experiences strengthen the neural networks around certain events. Over the course of 3–8 years old, the brain refines the motor, sensory, and language areas of the brain by pruning synapses that are unnecessary or unused. This development results in increased speed of processing, memory, and problem-solving for children 6–8 years old (Bergen, 2015). From 8 to 12 years of age, the frontal lobe of the brain continues to develop through myelination (i.e., pruning process) leading to greater processing speed and efficiency (Bergen, 2015). Brain development marks the development of elaborate, complex play as children grow older. Although a child's brain can develop strong neural pathways linking new experiences with old, the brain also retains neuroplasticity allowing connectivity to change in light of new experiences (Badenoch, 2018).

Neural connectivity is one aspect of the brain that helps us to understand how a child is taking in experiences. Here is one example of how this may work. A mother creates a nightly ritual in which she holds her young child in her lap and reads to her. Then the mother gives her child a hug and kiss before bed. The child experiences this event repeatedly and feels loved and nurtured during the event each time. When the child enters school, the Kindergarten teacher announces that there will be a storytelling time each day. The child is immediately excited and filled with positive emotions even before the story time because reading is connected with feelings of love and nurturance. The child does not consciously equate her mother's reading with the upcoming reading from her teacher. Her brain has created a neural network matching reading with a pleasant experience eliciting a positive expectation of the event. You can see how this type of neural networking would work quite differently for children who have survived adverse childhood experiences.

In addition to understanding neural network development, the structure of the brain contributes to our understanding of children. The three structures of the brain of which we are most concerned are the brainstem, limbic, and cortex. The brainstem controls the basic bodily functions such as breathing, sleeping, and blood flow. The brainstem is also closest to the spinal cord and sends messages back and forth between the brain and body (Badenoch, 2008). The center of the brain is the limbic region and includes the amygdala, hippocampus, and hypothalamus, among other structures. This part of the brain is known as the social brain and is focused on our emotional, relational, and memory experiences. The cerebral cortex is comprised of four lobes and is the center of our reasoning and regulation. In development, the brainstem is formed and ready to go prior to birth; the limbic system is formed at birth yet neural networks have yet to be developed; and the cortex is nascent at birth yet continues to grow throughout childhood into early adulthood (Badenoch, 2008). The brain works in coordination with the autonomic nervous system which extends from the head to the visceral organs and regulates bodily functions through its connectivity to the body. The autonomic nervous system responds to signals from both the environment and the body's organs (Porges, 2021). In a state of safety, the system supports the calm functioning of the body yet when under a perceived threat, the system activates to send messages of defense to the body which may include increased heart rate, hormone releases, physical tension, and restricted blood flow.

Cortisol is a hormone released by the brain as part of the body's stress-response system. Although cortisol releases are a normal part of daily functioning, too much cortisol released in the body indicates a stress response and leads to dysregulation in bodily functions, emotions, and behaviors. In stressful school environments, children have been shown to have an increase in cortisol.

Children who have experienced multiple adverse childhood experiences or complex trauma have been shown to respond to stressful events whereby the child's allostatic load (i.e., cumulative response to a threat) activates the body's stress-response system for a prolonged period of time resulting in damaging changes to endocrine, immunological, and other biological systems (Hays-Grudo & Morris, 2020; Waite & Ryan, 2020).

Play is one way that researchers have found that moves the body from a defense state to a calm and socially engaging state (Porges, 2021). Play with others triggers what is called neuroception which is the brain's unconscious awareness of environmental features that send messages of safety versus threat. Neuroception interprets the intentions of others through face, voice, gestures, and movements (Porges, 2021). In play, the child is able to perceive the safety of the environment and the play partner, thereby regulating the nervous system. Porges (2021) referred to play as a neural exercise that triggers neuroception. Badenoch (2008; 2018) further explained that play with a supportive adult supports the release of endogenous opioids, oxytocin, and dopamine which saturate the system with positive emotions and support relational connection. Hatfield & Williford (2017) concluded that participation in a play-based relational intervention between teacher and child resulted in lower levels of cortisol for preschool children. Play also supports the building of new neural networks through the connection of the pleasurable experience of play with relationship-building with the adult. Children are able to participate in new experiences that build trust, safety, and self-concept within the play setting; thereby creating new neural links between the experience of play, self, and other.

The following is an example of putting the brain information in action for greater understanding. Mariella is a third grader in Ms. Hodges' class. Mariella was adopted 2 years ago at the age of 6. Prior to her adoption, Mariella's mother surrendered custody when Mariella was 3 years old due to substance addiction. Mariella then lived in multiple foster homes before being adopted by two parents who appear to be eager to provide Mariella with a warm, loving home. It is November of the school year and up to this point, Ms. Hodges has developed a close, nurturing relationship with Mariella. Mariella occasionally has small, angry outbursts but they are manageable when Ms. Hodges talks her through these events. On Monday, Mariella arrives at school to learn that Ms. Hodges is absent due to having a cold. At this time, Mariella's nervous system is activated by the perception of threat. Threat messages are immediately perceived by the limbic system as a danger to Mariella. In Mariella's neural network, she unconsciously perceives the absence of Ms. Hodges as connected to the loss of her mother and continued disruptions in her attachment figures during her foster home placements. As a result of this activation, Mariella's brain floods her system with cortisol resulting in a burst of uncontrolled energy. Her heart rate rises and her breathing becomes uneven. As she walks to her desk, she trips and falls. She begins to cry and scream uncontrollably for what appears to be no reason at all. The substitute teacher, Ms. Adams, immediately responds to Mariella by taking her to a small play area in the classroom that includes many different toys and materials. Using a soothing voice, Ms. Adams introduces the area to Mariella by stating, "Mariella, here are toys and space you can play in." Ms. Adams continues to use a soothing voice while seeking eye contact and giving Mariella a warm smile. Through the process of neuroception, Mariella feels a sense of safety in the smaller play area designed for her developmental level and perceives nurturance from Ms. Adams who continues to send non-verbal messages of calm and support. Slowly, Mariella's physical symptoms become more regulated. As Mariella becomes more regulated, she engages reasoning through her prefrontal cortex and asks, "When will Ms. Hodges be back?" Ms. Adams answers with assurance, "I think she will be back in a couple of days but I will definitely be here each day until she gets back." As a result of this interaction, Mariella has experienced a new connection between events. Instead of the old neural pathway in which absence meant abandonment and fear, a new, albeit weaker, pathway is being forged in which absence is only an absence and not an existential threat as originally perceived by Mariella's brain and body. When enough alternate experiences of safety occur for Mariella, her neural pathway will become more well-established, leading to greater regulation.

The Developmental Path

Children develop along typical timelines with expected and predictable tasks, age characteristics, and challenges. Although each child is unique and will approach their developmental path based on biological and environmental factors, research has shown that we can expect for children to present in a fairly anticipated trajectory throughout childhood. Early childhood is characterized by rapid growth in development, demonstrating big changes at 6-month increments (Gesell Institute of Child Development, 2011). Beginning about the age of 7, growth slows down a bit but considerable transformation continues in the coming years. Table 3.1 provides a brief summary of typical characteristics, play behaviors, and challenges for each age of childhood. It should be noted that descriptions of ages are based on observations of typically developing children. Many children will follow at a different pace than the age groups listed, and children with complex histories or unique circumstances may look very different in their development. The purpose of sharing this quick guide to development is to highlight that children are rapidly developing and have various strengths, challenges, and play behaviors based on their age. Understanding what behaviors are predictable at specific ages helps to manage teacher expectations of how children are likely to think, feel, and act based on their development. Such understanding increases a teacher's empathic appreciation of children's worldviews. Table 3.1 also matches developmental characteristics with typical play behaviors in order to demonstrate how children will reveal their worlds developmentally in their play behaviors.

The relationship between play and development intersects specific areas that are critical to childhood wellness including self-regulation and social competence. Throughout development, children are using play to master and learn regulation of the self and the role and skills related to the social system. Understanding holistic child development requires the awareness of how play contributes to the development of self-regulation and social competencies.

Table 3.1 *Development At-A-Glance*

Age	Typical Characteristics	Play Behaviors	Normal Challenges
3	• Brain is 2 ½ times more active than adult brain • Speaks in sentences between 3 and 6 words • Enjoys repetition, rhymes, and new words • Able to walk, run, jump, and climb with ease • Experiences emotions with intensity • Begins to identify peers as friends	• Loves playing with other children • May prefer to play alone to avoid peer conflicts • Plays make-believe with dolls, animals, and playmates • Has a vivid fantasy life • Plays until exhausted • Is often silly and enjoys laughing • Has difficulty in cooperative play • Imitates others in play • Wants to wear costumes • Favors water play	• Has difficulty sharing • Struggles with problem-solving skills • Struggles to regulate emotions when tired • Often aggressive during playtime • Frequent potty training accidents • Masturbating in public • Enjoys being naked

(Continued)

Age	Typical Characteristics	Play Behaviors	Normal Challenges
3 1/2	• Major changes in vision and depth perception • Less coordinated • Determined and strong-willed • Expresses emotions more intensely	• Likes to play with friends • May have imaginary friends • Lots of imagination and inventiveness • Loves sandplay	• Cries, whines, or more difficulty separating from parents • Becomes more aggressive and defiant • Seems overly sensitive • Sucking thumb, picking nose, or chewing on clothes to self-soothe
4	• Experiencing peak period of brain development • Has a short attention span • Expanding vocabulary • Learns best by doing • Maintains high energy level • Likes to explore body • Strong feelings, both happy and sad • Likes to talk but not listen • Develops stronger friendships with peers	• Engages in dramatic, imaginative play with roles and stories • Loves dressing up • Needs lots of room to move • Takes initiative • Enjoys singing and dancing	• Tells fantastical lies • Struggles to distinguish fact from fiction • Can be aggressive and bossy • Lies when in trouble • Constant motion and noise

Age	Typical Characteristics	Play Behaviors	Normal Challenges
4 1/2	• Loves to learn new information • Having friends becomes important • Cooperative if not pressured • Shows interest in letters and numbers • Becoming more competent in skills	• Plays collaboratively with others • Starts to distinguish between fantasy and reality with greater ease • Likes to show off dramatically • Loves to play roles and assign roles to others	• Often fearful or anxious • May have frequent nightmares • May develop phobias • Inconsistent moods
5	• Masters simple planning and organization • Learns best through repetition • Sees only one way to do things • Gains more control over body movements • Calm and confident • Enjoys routine and predictability • Avoids overstimulation • Likes to help and cooperate • Eager to please	• Ascribes life to inanimate objects • Enjoys storytelling, imaginative play, and being creative • Engages other children in play and conversation • Plays well with others • Relates imaginative play to real life	• Enjoys screen time and needs limits • Lies to avoid punishment • Steals from others • Tattles • Becomes overwhelmed with choices • Can easily be dominated to please others

(Continued)

Age	Typical Characteristics	Play Behaviors	Normal Challenges
5 ½	• Questions and desires explanations • Gives more elaborate answers to questions • More restless and disorganized • Indecisive • Increasingly empathic toward others	• Can be oppositional when playing with others • Plays well in one moment, argues the next • Enjoys imaginative play with roles and stories • Relates imaginative play to real life	• Struggles to keep balance physically • May seem overly demanding and disobedient • Complains frequently • Becomes easily overwhelmed
6	• Increased ability to focus • Can follow more complicated directions • Loves to ask questions • Learns in an environment of noise and movement • Moves with speed and high energy but tires easily • Proud of accomplishments • Wants to be best and first at everything • Values friends and picks friends who are similar • Affectionate and friendly with teachers • Seeks independence	• Differentiates between fantasy and reality • Enjoys telling and hearing stories • Interested in competency and mastery • Often wrestles, chases, or screams when playing	• Complains about aches and pains • Highly sensitive to criticism and correction • Lies to avoid punishment • Does not admit when wrong • Poor sport • Often cheats or changes rules to win • Bedtime fears • Bedwetting during times of stress • Argumentative, especially about autonomy

Age	Typical Characteristics	Play Behaviors	Normal Challenges
6 ½	• Likes sharing new knowledge and skills • Slows down from earlier speed • Calmer and more easygoing • Likes to try new things • Enjoys intellectual tasks • Warm and loving • Gets along well with teachers and parents	• Loves playing guessing games • Sense of humor • Enjoys cooperative play • Creates competitive games • Enjoys playing with language	• Extreme sensitivity to criticism • High levels of activity • Performance anxiety • Lies to win or get out of trouble
7	• Highly observant of others • Better impulse control • Understands irony and sarcasm • Stronger reasoning abilities • Stronger hand-eye coordination • Sensitive to others' feelings • Likes to follow rules	• Cooperative in play • Concerned with competency, possibly perfectionistic • May move to have more inner dialogue in play • Enjoys setting up challenges • Sets up rules for play	• Often more withdrawn and quieter • May seem moody without cause • Increased worries, especially about serious events such as war and disasters • Sensitive to rejection

(Continued)

Age	Typical Characteristics	Play Behaviors	Normal Challenges
8	• Gains in long-term memory • Converses more maturely and adjusts language for context • High energy • Good fine motor skills • Outgoing and sociable • Spends increased time with friends • Influenced by peers • Can understand and interpret others' emotions • Can self-regulate • Concerned with fairness	• Enjoys humor and playing jokes on others • Builds and takes things apart to see how they work • Enjoys high energy activities • Likes competitive play • Prefers to play with others rather than solitary play • Enjoys games and art	• Self-critical and self-competitive • Increased concerns about peer acceptance • Testing rules and limits for autonomy • Can be rude and demanding
9	• Enjoys mastering skills independently • Thinks logically and rationally • More detail-oriented and self-sufficient • Desires more privacy • Determined and motivated • Can take the perspective of others • Concerned with social groups and peer acceptance	• Decreased interest in fairy tales, fables, and magic • Enjoys rough and tumble play, mostly for boys • Enjoys physical activity and organized sports • Prefers play with peers but can be overly competitive • Free play is mixed with verbal conversation	• Complains frequently about aches and pains • Tends to worry or become anxious • Tends to be perfectionistic • May seem detached or disinterested in parents • Struggle with school performance anxiety • Competitiveness with others • Avoidance of activities they believe they are likely to fail

Age	Typical Characteristics	Play Behaviors	Normal Challenges
10	• Thinks logically and concretely • Increased processing speed • Likes active learning approaches • Increased speed, power, and accuracy • Flexible and easygoing • Uses cognitive skills to regulate emotions • Cooperative • Seeks out support through friendships • Takes on values and norms of identified group	• Enjoys playing in groups • Mixes free play with organized play • Enjoys rules and follows rules set in play • Enjoys constructive and mastery play	• Excessive concern with belonging to the group • Choosing peer values over family values • Can become angry quickly • Group identity may take precedence over self-identity
11	• Increased deductive reasoning skills • Prefers to learn new skills rather than mastering old ones • Likes to discuss ideas and practice logic • Is more internally focused and self-involved • Strong sense of fairness • Challenges or questions rules • Defines identity by peer group • Enjoys working in collaborative groups • Interested in sexual and romantic relationships	• Likes to move and engage in activity • Prefers play with peers but social disruptions are likely • Enjoys constructive play – building things • Enjoys artistic play – creating things	• Experiences more frequent illnesses, may complain of headaches • Tend to be self-conscious about body changes • Moody and unpredictable • Easily frustrated • Argumentative and can be cruel to peers • Argumentative with adults • High sensitivity to being corrected in front of others

(Continued)

Age	Typical Characteristics	Play Behaviors	Normal Challenges
12	• Craves brain stimulation and novelty • Developing ability for abstract thinking • Sensitive to body changes among peers • Needs substantial amounts of food, sleep, and exercise • Enthusiastic • Unpredictable and hard to read • Experiment with different ways of being or acting • Spends more time socializing with peers and less with family • Strives to be equal to peers	• Likes to move and engage in activity • Prefers play with peers but social disruptions are likely • Enjoys constructive play – building things • Enjoys artistic play – creating things	• Overly sensitive about appearance and performance • Engages in gossip • Lacks motivation for schoolwork • Growing interest in sex and romantic relationships • Excluding some peers to fit in with others • Challenging rules and authority figures

Note: Much of the information from this table was gathered from Ray's (2016) *A therapist guide to child development: The extraordinarily normal years.*

4
Play and Self-Regulation

Self-regulation is a topic of concern for school professionals and a common goal of school mental health or character education curriculums. Self-regulation, alternately referred to as emotional regulation, is a state of being in which a child is physically, cognitively, emotionally, and socially calm and composed. All aspects are integrated, and the child is operating from a place of self-control and self-monitoring. We often talk about self-regulation as a verb: Can a child regulate themselves? Is a child regulated? How do we help a child regulate? We set self-regulation as a goal because children who are regulated can engage in higher order thought processes, refrain from impulsivity, demonstrate emotional stability, and use more favorable social skills. Children who are more self-regulated are likely to perform better on academic tasks, have better quality and number of peer relationships, are less likely to engage in risky behaviors, and enjoy greater mental health overall. Self-regulation, to be sure, is a worthy goal for child development.

The Brain and Self-Regulation

Earlier, in Chapter 3, I addressed brain development which is critical to the development of self-regulation. For self-regulation to occur, the autonomic nervous system sends message of calm throughout the body. When the autonomic system is perceived under threat, messages of alarm are sent

DOI: 10.4324/9781003285618-6

throughout the body through restricted blood flow, increased heart rate, shallow breathing, overwhelming thoughts or possibly no thoughts at all, and an instinct to remove self from the situation through the flight, fight, or freeze response (Porges, 2021). When children are dysregulated, they will respond from instincts to (a) fight (e.g., child kicks teacher when told to sit down at desk); (b) flight (e.g., child runs from room when the teacher says it's time for a math test); or (c) freeze (e.g., child seems to not hear or see teacher after hitting a classmate). Dysregulation is usually accompanied by an inability to engage in prefrontal cortex operations. The limited access to cortex processes of the brain is the reason that Anisha is unable to answer the teacher's questions about her reason for hitting another child or coming to school with no coat for recess. When a teacher asks an 8-year-old to answer "why" questions, the child is required to access the rational center of the brain. When a child perceives threat, other parts of the brain (e.g., limbic system) and autonomic nervous system are online while the prefrontal cortex is offline. This is not a time to reason, it is a time to protect or defend for survival.

I propose that most teachers are sensitive to a child's brain processes as a natural reaction to being threatened. I believe the misunderstanding and miscommunication occurs around what a child perceives as a threat versus what a teacher perceives as a threat. In many discussions with teachers, I have heard examples such as, "I just asked her to sit down, and then she started screaming," "He was laughing one minute, and then started tearing pictures off the wall the next," "We were watching a movie, and afterward he just sat there ignoring me." On the surface level, none of these incidents would be perceived as a threat by most adults. The teacher's confusion is real and makes sense. The part that is typically unknown is how the child perceives the event. Imagine the following scenarios related to the above examples.

Anisha, in fourth grade, is worried about the reading comprehension test. She knows that she is behind her peers in reading and her grades are low, possibly failing. If she does not do well on this test, she will have to go into extra classes for reading, and all of her friends will believe she is not as smart as them. She has been anxious about this test for the last 3 three days and now it is time. Just a minute before the test, Anisha's pencil breaks. She jumps up to borrow a pencil from another classmate. Anisha's teacher is not aware of Anisha's pencil break and tells Anisha firmly to sit down for the test. Anisha reacts by screaming, "You hate me. I hate you more." The teacher is shocked by such an out-of-proportion reaction. Anisha's limbic system perceives an existential threat to belonging in her peer group and her self-concept. She is unable to access the part of the brain which would problem-solve a solution of calmly explaining the situation to the teacher.

Robert, in second grade, lives with his single mother, who is harsh with Robert. Robert's mother is not physically abusive, but when he makes a mistake, her punishment is that he must go somewhere else in the house alone, and she will not talk to him for hours. Robert equates getting in trouble with being lonely and unloved (i.e., neural connections). Robert has just come in from recess with his class. He had a wonderful time at recess, played with all of his friends, and even won the race. He is boisterous and energetic. The teacher gives him a stern look, attempting to send him a message to calm down without calling him out or embarrassing him. Robert sees the teacher's face and immediately starts to run around the room, tearing papers off the wall. The simple act of neuroception (Robert seeing the look on the teacher's face) connected with his neural network (unhappy looks lead to loneliness) has led Robert's body to perceive threat and become dysregulated.

Alex, first grade, just transferred to the school this year and has been in three different schools over his last two school years. Alex's family has been investigated by Child Protective Services but he was not removed from the home. His mother recently left his father by going to the local domestic violence shelter. Alex is living in the shelter currently while his mother tries to find a job and a permanent home. During the movie at school that day, Alex accidentally fell asleep and he urinated on himself. When the movie was over, he realized his pants were wet. As soon as he realized the accident, his mind goes blank. He isn't having any thoughts or feelings that he can access. As the other students get up to go to their desks, the teacher tells Alex to go to his desk. Alex sits there blankly looking away as if he had not heard anything. In an annoyed voice, the teacher states the directive again and Alex appears to ignore her. The accident has set Alex's autonomic nervous system into full arrest based on a perceived threat of abuse and abandonment. In Alex's case, his systems are shutting down (picture a possum playing dead) because that is the best way the body has to protect itself under extreme threat.

In all of these cases, the child's perceived threat is relatively undetectable by the teacher, yet the threats lead to excessive cases of dysregulation. Rest assured, that if a child reacts in ways that seem out of proportion to the situation, the brain is registering a threat. In the moment, it is not necessary for the teacher to know the nature of the threat perceived by the child. The most important knowledge is that the child is not going to engage as if the prefrontal cortex is fully functioning. The child will be responding as if a threat is occurring. The teacher's role is then to respond in ways that calm and regulate the child's system. The teacher's response is one path to helping children learn to self-regulate.

How Does Play Contribute to Self-Regulation?

Connecting the dots between play and self-regulation requires going back to understanding the development of play for children. In imaginative play, children are given the opportunity to structure their own worlds and their own scenarios. In early childhood years, structure is imposed on to the child by adults and children learn the rules of others. Very young children follow rules faithfully and take on the structures of situations from others. They know rules based on the structures around them. If I cry, I will be fed so I will cry when I'm hungry. If I yell, my father will take away my toy so I will not yell. Around the age of 3, children grow in their need for autonomy and develop an interest in questioning rules that have hitherto gone unquestioned. This questioning usually starts in children's play. During play, the child begins to explore and make their own rules. This starts very simply with a 3-year-old imitating rules of adults. A typical play behavior at that age: We eat and then we clean the kitchen. By 4-years old, children are experimenting with rules for people behaviors through their dramatic play. A typical play behavior at that age: The family of lions is hungry. The mom and dad lion go to get the food. The baby lion is happy that they will be bringing back food. The baby lion's job is to set the table for dinner when mom and dad get back. In this scenario, the 4-year-old is playing with ideas of rules associated with roles. In this play, the baby lion could be assigned any role but the child has designated the role of the baby lion to follow the rules of being happy and helping. These are the beginnings of self-regulation. Nicolopoulou (2019) highlighted Vygotsky's theory that play is where children first impose their own rules on their activity. This movement to explore self-constraint and its consequences results in building self-regulation.

As children grow older, their play becomes more intricate, and rules become more complex. The 6-year-old might create play scenes with rules provided for multiple roles and rules may be changed as the child experiments with outcomes. Another self-regulation process in play can be seen in the use of materials. A 3- or 4-year-old will typically use a whole bottle of glue if given the opportunity while a 6-year-old will attempt to save some for next time. Older children will continue to grow in their restraint based on how much glue is needed for their project to come out as they desire. There is a dance back and forth for children as they learn to negotiate their needs and their resources resulting in growth in their abilities to regulate their actions to meet their needs.

Older children (7–12 years) extend the exploration of rules to peers and more structured games. At these ages, children like to invent games and experiment with the changing and implementation of rules. An 8-year-old will draw a standing line for throwing a ball into the hoop. If that becomes too easy or too hard, the child may experiment with changing the line but the rule will remain that you have to stay at the line. Such a rule encourages self-regulation based on imposed rules. As older children grow in their social needs, they learn to experiment with rules in the context of others' rules. The intersection of rules and peers is where children learn to self-regulate socially to meet their relational needs. How do I control my anger when I am frustrated by my friend's rules? Children actually practice this skill in their play.

The key to the development of self-regulation through play is that children are organically designed to experiment with these ideas across early and later childhood. Given a self-directed play environment, children innately desire to explore the idea of regulating themselves in their living environments. This is why children play "school" and play "house." Through their play, they are figuring out how to best function within their circumstances. They learn that their emotions, thoughts, and actions are intertwined and have consequences. And the amazing part is that they learn all of this through their own curiosity and drive, without adult direction to do so.

Research supports the link between play and self-regulation. Veiga et al. (2016) noted that preschoolers decreased in disruptive behaviors following increased time for free play while Russ et al. (2011) summarized research supporting the link between imaginative play and emotional regulation. In my own research in play therapy (see Attachment A), I have explored the impact of play therapy on the self-regulation of children across ages and presenting issues. Given a self-directed play environment and a safe relationship with a therapist, children across age groups show improvement in self-regulation. We have mostly explored the indicators of improved self-regulation including aggressive, disruptive, and externalizing behaviors. For children that present with clinical levels of aggression, autistic children, children with multiple adverse childhood experiences, participation in play therapy has resulted in decreases in problem behaviors. In fact, the most consistent finding we have in the world of play therapy is that play therapy reduces children's actions of acting out, hurting self and others, and disrupting their environments. And yet, we do not directly teach children self-regulation skills in play therapy. Furthermore, the research on teacher-child play (see Attachment B) indicates that children who participate in self-directed play sessions with their teachers decrease their problem behaviors in the classroom. Our findings are a confirmation that children work toward better emotional regulation when they are provided with the opportunity to play in safe environments.

What Does Self-Regulation Look Like in Play?

Using our knowledge of brain processes, relationship variables, play, and child development, we can start to pull together a picture of how self-regulation improves through play. The ability of children to grow and connect through the language of play provides them with the opportunity to lower their stress about having to understand and communicate in a world that is foreign to them, the verbal adult world. The provision of play allows children to let their guard down so that they may begin to explore their emotions and actions on their own terms. Additionally, when children engage in the process of play, the brain releases chemicals (e.g., dopamine) that send messages of safety and peace to the body. As the body is relaxed and not under threat, the child can explore thoughts, emotions, and behaviors more freely. They are free to try out their creative ideas for coping skills to regulate their emotions.

Play in relationship is especially salient to building self-regulation skills. When a child plays in relationship with an adult, there are several dynamics taking place that encourage self-regulation. First, the very act of an adult spending time with a child on the child's terms sends a powerful message that the child is worthy of such presence. Self-regulation is often undermined by a child's deep feeling of disconnectedness and insignificance. Many children rarely experience times in which an adult is interested in them without distraction and willing to follow their lead. This presence is interpreted by the child as I am worthy, I am of value, I am important which translates in a stronger self-concept. Second, the warmth and nurturance of an adult during play provides the child with feelings of being fully accepted. Feeling fully accepted, the child is under no threat to be a certain way or act in ways that are pleasing to the adult. When children feel pressured to change, they will often react with big emotions and actions. It is when children feel fully accepted, they experience the freedom to change through peaceful exploration.

Finally, play in the presence of a caring adult sends the message to the child that they are not alone. As the child experiences the tone, expressions, and openness provided by the adult (i.e., neuroception), along with verbal responses to engage and understand the child's play, the relationship built provides the child with a regulatory partner. That partner serves as a person with whom the child can attune to for co-regulation. This co-regulation role is an essential one for a teacher in play and classroom interaction. The teacher's self-regulation is critical to the child's ability to regulate. The child looks to the teacher to decide when situations are safe and how to react to events. A teacher who is dysregulated likely leads to a child who is dysregulated. Playful activities for co-regulation are shared in Chapter 13. In play, the teacher and child regulate through their attunement to one another and their mutual attention and focus to the child's play.

We expect children to learn regulation through the co-regulation process during infancy with primary caretakers. However, many children do not experience the parent-child relationship necessary to build these capacities. These children enter elementary school with a lack of emotional support, past experiences of regulation, and models of regulation. The teacher's model of self-regulation may be the child's only opportunity to engage the brain in the process and learn these skills. Play provides the medium through which the child can focus on regulatory attunement with an adult without the myriad of distractions that can derail the regulation process.

Self-regulation is a prerequisite for warm and nurturing relationships. We see this in classrooms when a child who is aggressive, frequently crying, or overly intrusive or disruptive suffers, not only from chaotic emotions, but also struggles with having friends. Typically regulated children are often overwhelmed by children who have big emotions and big behaviors. Adults are also sometimes overwhelmed by frequently dysregulated children and will respond with relational disconnection. The link between play and self-regulation appears to be intricately linked to social ability.

5

Play and Social Relationships

Social awareness and mastery are threaded throughout a child's play in both solitary and group play. When a primary caregiver gives a toy to an infant, the infant is likely to move their eyes from the person to the object and back, looking for signs of connection between the object, the caregiver, and the infant. Play interactions are embedded in social context. As early as 2 years, a child's pretend play takes on interpersonal skills of reciprocal social interaction (Jent et al., 2011). Smith (2010) highlighted research supporting the social aspect of play including Haight and Miller's (1993) finding that when children were observed at home, up to 75% of their pretend play was social in nature even when playing alone. Sociodramatic play, in which a child imagines or acts out roles of people or animals, begins in toddlerhood, and grows in frequency and sustained play over the next few years (Nicolopoulou, 2019). Humans are social animals and children start from the beginning with an interest in mastering the social world.

Development of Social Play

In early imaginative play, 3-year-olds take on play that imitates roles they have observed in others, such as cooking, cleaning, and building. This play indicates that children are keen observers of adults and other children as their first foray into their social worlds. They practice in their play the actions they have observed in their worlds, particularly the actions of people with whom

DOI: 10.4324/9781003285618-7

they have the most contact. At this young age, children associate family roles with actions and their play is likely to represent these actions. This play helps young children figure out their place of belonging in their family structures and the roles they play in interactions with family members.

In less than a year later, preschoolers move to sociodramatic play, also known as imaginative or make-believe play, in which social roles are assigned within play scenes. This type of play allows the child to take on various roles of social play. The 4- and 5-year-old child will often assign roles to others if they are playing within a group or personify inanimate objects with a social role if playing alone. The cow is assigned a name and a personality that inter-acts with the cat who also has a name and personality. Imaginative play allows the child to try out various social scenarios wherein the cow and cat figure out how to be friends or decide to be enemies. There is an interplay between characters when the child places them in multiple social scenarios. In each scene, the child is learning and setting the rules for social interactions. This sociodramatic play also introduces one of the basic skills for social success: the ability to take on others' perspectives. It is in this early imaginative play that children start to imagine that one character thinks one way and another character thinks a different way. The awareness that multiple perspectives exist and the ability to see another's perspective is referred to as theory of mind. In early play, a child develops the first building block for empathy which is knowing that different people think different ways.

Imagine a simple and everyday play scene. Rory, a 4-year-old, sets up a scene with a spider and a rabbit. She names the spider, Crawley, and the rabbit is assigned the name, Jumpy. Rory moves the spider through the sand saying, "Crawley is scared and hiding so that he can get home. Then, he runs right into Jumpy." Rory moves Jumpy up and down in a quick, scared manner.

> Jumpy screams. He is scared of Crawley. Crawley says, 'don't be scared. I'm your friend.' Jumpy says, 'are you sure you're my friend? You are sneaky.' Crawley says, 'I'm really nice. I just hide so I don't get stepped on.' Jumpy says, 'okay you can be my friend.'

In this simple illustration, we can see Rory laying the groundwork for taking on different perspectives. She gives intentions to both characters that differ from one another. She recognizes that both characters meet each other but see each other differently through their own perspective. This is the begin-ning of theory of mind work. As Rory plays out scenes in which characters reveal their unique perspectives, Rory is learning that she sees things her way and others might see it a different way. Other children or adults might have their own thoughts that are different than Rory's. Because young children are relatively egocentric and assume their thoughts are the same as those around them, this play is what leads them to the necessary social skill of knowing that others think differently.

The follow-up to theory of mind is the development of empathy. Once children know that people have different ways of thinking, they start to imagine that people must also have different ways of feeling. If I can think what a person is thinking, the next step is to practice feeling what they are feeling. Going back to Rory's play scene, Crawley sees that Jumpy is scared and tries to soothe Jumpy's fears by saying, "Don't be scared." If we carefully read this play scene, we will notice that Jumpy never *said* she was scared. Crawley saw that Jumpy screamed and jumped up and down. Crawley *saw* that Jumpy was scared. In Rory's mind, she was able to act out the scene in a way that Jumpy revealed she was scared without saying it and Crawley was able to pick up the fear and respond to it. We now see that Rory is not only building theory of mind but is also building her awareness of empathy, as well as social skills to use to share empathy. Through pretend play, children are given the opportunity to experience their emotional states and imagine the states of others (Jent et al., 2011). If we are keenly observing, we can see the mastery and complexity of children's play scenes in their contribution toward social-emotional growth.

The process of perspective-taking, feeling for others, and developing skills to respond to these awarenesses takes time. The 4-year-old is just starting the process. From ages 6 to 9, children are focused on adapting to demands of a social world (Elkind, 2007). Play becomes a highly social activity and as elementary age children grow older, there is less of a need for object play as children become increasingly socially reciprocal in their pretend play (Jent et al., 2011). Objects are replaced by real peers and roles are taken on with a perspective different from only a single child who directs solitary play scenes. Children must now navigate through multiple perspectives. In pretend play, children are regularly signaling to each other through body movements and facial expressions leading to more nuanced ability to read social interactions (Jent et al., 2011). Children often engage in physical play and movements to master how to give and receive signals accurately.

Rough and tumble play is one type of play in which it is most obvious that children are experimenting with limits to aggression and physical touch. In rough and tumble play, two children will move toward one another sending signals of play such as smiles, nods, open body postures. When they engage in physical play, there might be laughter or screams of delight. When one child pushes too hard, there is usually a signal such as deeper-toned shout, a silence, or facial expression change that signals to the child that the play has gone too far and is no longer fun. In response, the child who pushed too hard readjusts and re-engages with a lighter push. The child who signaled hurt responsively re-engages and the play begins again. A tremendous amount of social learning takes place in rough and tumble play. Although rough and tumble play is seen most frequently in boys, girls are likely to experiment with touch signals outside of rough and tumble play. Girls may engage in relational touch aggression such as grabbing a friend's hand to lead them, or trying to dress up a friend too vigorously. Just as in rough and tumble play, the peer may pull back their hand or move away from the dress-up to send a signal that the child's physical touch is too intrusive. These physical play interactions are part of the social learning process and signify the need for these types of play opportunities.

Again, interactive play among peers spurs growth of a child's empathy. When a child pushes too hard, they can see that the other child is hurt or unhappy. When a child watches a peer build a wall that crumbles immediately, the child can see that their peer is frustrated. In the play environment, the child is exposed to others' feeling and thoughts frequently. In an environment where each child is safe and accepted by an adult, empathy is likely to be developed between children. The natural response is for the child to recognize the other child's feelings and respond accordingly. Responses may include reaching out to help or simply sitting beside their peer as they are sad. In safe play environments, awareness and responsiveness are more likely to occur because each child's perceived level of threat is low and thereby, the child is able to access multiple cognitive abilities including perspective-taking and problem-solving. In play spaces where an adult is also providing empathic understanding, children experience both feelings of empathy from the adult and observe modeling of empathic responses. The building of empathy builds relational connections between children that serve to grow and enhance friendships.

In older childhood, games are the dominant play activity between children. It is through creating games with rules, a typical play behavior of older elementary students, that children learn social skills, attitudes, and values (Elkind, 2007). Games require negotiation between children. Negotiation ensues because the ultimate goal is to keep the game going. If a child insists on playing a game only their way, they will likely lose the opportunity to keep playing with other children. This social aspect involves several intricate processes. First, the child is engaging in theory of mind and empathy. The child sees that her fellow peer wants to play the game differently and there is value in the child's perspective. The child sees that her peer is determined that the game must be played this way and empathizes with the importance the peer has placed on this game. Secondly, when the child is developing optimally, the child experiences a strong sense of self and values their ways of doing things. Next, the child is then faced with the social dilemma of "my needs versus my friend's needs." This dilemma may lead to frustration and anger which must be regulated by the child in order to keep the play going. Self-regulation is integral to the social skill process. In the midst of valuing their peer, valuing self, experiencing internal conflict, and resulting emotions, the child then engages in the social skills of negotiation. All of this is going on during what appears to be a simple recess game of "leader of the mountain" for a group of 8-year-olds. If navigated successfully, there are compromises, everyone stays friends, and the game continues. If not navigated successfully, there are usually upset feelings and loss of the game. But there is always tomorrow's recess when the children get to practice the social nuances and skills again. There is simply no way to teach this type of learning directly with the depth of complexities involved. Play allows children to work toward social skills in real time and with real consequences.

Social Skills Play in Action

In looking at the research (Attachment A), we see that social skills are heavily influenced by self-directed therapeutic play experiences. Social competence is built through play experiences with peers and in individual play therapy. Recently, I observed a series of play therapy sessions with a group of two second grade boys, Devon and Aaron, who had been referred for aggression and lack of friends. The following is an excerpt from an early session. The boys and the therapist entered the playroom.

DEVON (IMMEDIATELY GRABS THE SHIELD AND SWORD): *I got it first, you can't have it.*

AARON (CLEARLY BOTHERED BUT PRETENDS NOT TO BE): *I don't care.*

THERAPIST: *Devon, you're excited about those and you don't want Aaron to have it. And Aaron you're saying you just don't care.*

AARON (SMILES WHEN HE SEES ANOTHER SWORD. HE GRABS IT): *See, I got one! (He then takes a swing at Devon. Although it doesn't hit him, Devon screams loudly).*

THERAPIST: *Aaron you're happy about the sword but Devon isn't for hitting. You can hit the chair with the sword. Devon, you're mad about almost getting hit.*

DEVON (STILL UPSET): *I don't care. Aaron, you're stupid.*

THERAPIST: *Devon you're upset but people aren't for calling stupid. You can say you're mad.*

AARON: *Well, you're stupider. You're the most stupid.*

THERAPIST: *Aaron, you're upset too but people aren't for calling stupid. You can say you're mad at Devon.*

The session went on similarly for 30 minutes with each child attempting to get a better toy and insulting the other child. Because of the arguing and limit-setting, neither child was able to enjoy their playtime with each other or even play on their own in any satisfying way. The therapist remained regulated and modeled regulation for the boys. The therapist attempted to reflect each child's feelings so the child felt understood and cared for. The therapist provided ideas for alternative actions to let the children know they could find other ways to get their needs met. Both boys exhibited strong personalities with accompanying strong opinions and desires to be in charge. But they also exhibited a strong need to interact with one another indicating they had high social needs for relationships. One or both of them could have moved to a corner of the room and played alone but they both opted to continue to engage with one another even if it resulted in a negative interaction. In subsequent sessions, Devon and Aaron continued their competitive and negative interactions with glimpses of negotiations to allow for brief moments of collaborative play. Within an eight session time span, they created a game of "Slay the dragons." In order to slay the dragons, they decided that Devon would use the sword to stab the dragon and Aaron would use the bat to hit the dragon over the head. The following is an excerpt from their ninth play session:

DEVON: *I'm going to sneak up and stab him from behind.*

AARON: *No, no. I want to sneak up behind.*

DEVON: *It's my turn to do that. You go to the front of the dragon.*

AARON (SCOWLS AND MOVES AWAY FROM THE PLAY): *Then I'm not going to do anything.*

DEVON (DEFIANTLY): *I'll do it by myself. (Devon stabs the dragon with his sword and then looks at Aaron who is sitting on the other side of the room.) See I did it! (Aaron doesn't respond. Devon walks over to Aaron.) You can do it the next two times.*

AARON: (JUMPS UP WITH ENTHUSIASM): *I want to do it the next three times.*

DEVON (ALSO EXCITED): *Okay, the next 3 times. I'll jump in front to get him.*

In this scenario, you can see a marked difference in how the boys interact. Their personalities and preferences are still strong but they prioritize their desire to play together over their desire to control the play. Using nascent social skills, they have ceased calling each other names or attempting to be aggressive with one another. They start to notice each other's feelings. Devon realizes he made a mistake when Aaron disappointedly sits down. Aaron realizes how strongly Devon wants to play a certain way and instead of fighting removes himself in order to maintain his own regulation. They make attempts to negotiate so that they may return to the play. Devon physically moves closer to

Aaron to engage him and offers a peace offering of letting Aaron fight from behind the dragon. Aaron responds enthusiastically to the offer and counter offers with a reasonable solution. They both let go of the desire to win their battle with each other in order to play together. It is through this self-directed play interaction that the boys grow in their social skills and abilities to move to relational connection. At the same time, these play skills often transfer to other child environments. In the case of Devon and Aaron, both teachers reported a reduction in their aggression and a greater ability to get along with their classmates.

One of the perplexing findings from our research is that children in individual play sessions also demonstrate improved social skills and competence after participation in self-directed play therapy with a therapist. In fact, the same gains in social skills are reported in individual play and group play equally. Although it seems logical that when children are grouped together they are likely to work on social skills, the logic does not seem quite as obvious when the child is the only child in the session. These findings require a little more theoretical conjecture. One explanation for the positive growth of social skills in individual play sessions may be the connection between empathy and social competence. Empathy is an essential feature of relationships. Empathy allows us to recognize how others feel and to experience those feelings as our own. When we empathize in a relationship, we are intimately connected to another person in a way that sends messages of care and concern. In individual play sessions, the adult facilitator of play seeks to have full empathic understanding of the child and communicate this empathy to the child. The hope is that the child perceives this care and empathy in a way that the child feels understood and accepted, culminating in a feeling of worthiness. If this hope is realized, the child can now access their own levels of empathy based on their experiences of receiving empathy. They can now give away what they have received. In their everyday interactions with others, the child now initiates social interactions from a place of positive self-worth and the ability to share the empathy they have experienced. This attitude motivates the desire to interact socially and practice social skills. It is possible that the receiving and development of empathy are more essential to the process of social competence than the actual practice of social skills.

Across childhood, we can see that play is interwoven into all aspects of holistic development of the child. In summary of the findings presented, play accompanies the development of cognitive abilities including higher order thinking, problem-solving, language, and comprehension. Furthermore, play is linked to imagination, creativity, emotional expression, self-regulation, and coping skills. And finally, social attitudes and skills are nurtured and practiced through play. Research is mixed regarding the conclusion that play causes the development of these qualities but it is clear that play is the natural form of expression in the acquisition of these qualities. Play accompanies the child's development of thinking, feeling, and doing. Because children are intricately involved in the process of play throughout their process of development, play is a foundational activity for both education and relationship.

II

ACTIVATING THE POWERS OF PLAY BETWEEN TEACHER AND CHILD: THE PLAYBREAK

6

Bringing Together the Powers of Play to Activate Learning

In the 1960s, there was a particularly exciting new development in the world of play therapy: the discovery that play therapy skills could be taught to adults other than therapists to facilitate child relationships. Bernard Guerney (1964) introduced filial therapy to the mental health world, and the intervention was further developed by Louise Guerney (2000). Filial therapy is a mental health intervention designed to address childhood emotional and behavioral problems by training parents to serve as therapeutic agents for their children. Although some therapists at the time had shared cases of teaching parents play therapy skills to use with their children, Guerney and Guerney developed a process by which therapists could train parents in a more structured format to conduct play sessions. Because the parent-child relationship is the most influential relationship in a child's life, filial therapy seemed well-suited to facilitate the emotional wellness of children. Based on Child-Centered Play Therapy, filial therapy is grounded in the philosophy that relationship, acceptance, and play are key ingredients to building healthy relationships with children. Filial therapists teach parents the play therapy skills to use during play sessions with their children. Originally, filial therapy was conceived as a long-term intervention lasting approximately 1 year in which groups of parents serve as a support system for each other weekly while they are in training. Outcomes were quite positive with parents reporting increased levels of self-confidence in their parenting and reduced child behavior problems.

Filial therapy has continued to grow and thrive since its inception. Garry Landreth (2002) modified the structure of filial therapy to a 10-week model in which parents participate in weekly 2-hour group educational sessions

DOI: 10.4324/9781003285618-9

and facilitate weekly play sessions with their children. Sue Bratton and Garry Landreth continued to revise and explore the structure of filial therapy, culminating in the conception of Child-Parent Relationship Therapy (Bratton & Landreth, 2020; Landreth & Bratton, 2019). Both filial therapy and Child-Parent Relationship Therapy are supported by decades of research supporting the models as effective interventions for childhood behavioral and emotional problems, parent-child relationships stress, and parenting skills (Bratton et al., 2005; Lin & Bratton, 2015). The development and success of filial raised the question: Can teaching play therapy skills to other adults in children's lives result in similar positive outcomes?

Naturally, teachers became a focus early in the discovery of filial therapy. With a prolific amount of research substantiating the impact of child-teacher relationships, play therapists proposed the potential benefits of extending filial therapy to the school setting. At the same time, Guerney and Guerney were studying the effects of filial therapy on child-parent dyads, they were also expanding their work into the schools with teachers. Guerney and Flumen (1970) trained 11 elementary school teachers in Child-Centered Play Therapy and then examined the outcomes of teachers leading 14 play sessions with children who had been identified as withdrawn. The children who participated in play sessions with their teachers demonstrated higher levels of participation and assertiveness in the classroom. From this point, there were very few research reports of filial being conducted with teachers but anecdotal evidence indicates that school counselors continued to explore methods of how to implement filial within the increasingly crowded schedule of elementary schools.

That all changed when a research team out of Georgia State University led by JoAnna White, Mary Flynt, and Kay Draper (1997) introduced a modification to the filial model that integrated Child-Centered and Individual Psychology principles specifically designed to train teachers as therapeutic agents for children. Rather than sticking to the more rigid and lengthy model of filial and Child-Parent Relationship Therapy, White et al. proposed the Kinder Training Model could be presented in a modified format to better match the school environment. In the initial Kinder Training, teachers participated in a 1-day training where they were taught the skills of Child-Centered Play Therapy and Individual Psychology principles of logical consequences, goals of behavior, and encouragement (Nelsen et al., 2013; White et al., 1997). Following the 1-day training, the teachers began a series of 6 weekly play sessions with a child who was identified as benefitting from the intervention. The school counselor supported the teachers by sitting in on the first session and then reviewing recordings with the teachers from the subsequent five sessions. In studying the effects of Kinder Training, Draper et al. (2001)

found participating students decreased in classroom behavioral problems and improved literacy skills while teachers increased encouraging statements and effective limit-setting.

I was fortunate to attend a workshop presented by the Kinder Training team at the Association for Play Therapy Annual Conference in 1998. With my focus on play therapy in the schools, I had run into frustrations with using the 10-session filial model in schools. Although I was certain that filial for teachers was an untapped rich resource for teachers and children, the school schedule and demands on teachers were obstacles to implementing the model. The Kinder Training model was inspiring in seeing the creativity used in adapting the structure of the original filial model while maintaining the core principles of relationship and play. I was not the only one inspired. Within a few years, Phyllis Post and her team out of University of North Carolina-Charlotte had implemented the filial teacher model with her own adaptations, resulting in positive research outcomes indicating decreased child behavioral problems, increase in children's adaptive skills, and improved classroom skills for teachers (Post et al., 2004). Post's research teams have continued to refine the application of the filial teacher model with a particular focus on cultural outcomes related to the model (see Attachment B).

At the University of North Texas, our team has worked over the last two decades to modify the filial model for practical implementation in preschool and elementary school settings. Sue Bratton, Natalya Lindo, and I have led multiple research teams exploring methods and examining outcomes of what is typically referred to under the umbrella of Child Teacher Relationship Training (alternate terms include play-based teacher consultation, teacher-child relationship building, and Relationship Enhancement for Learner and Teacher). Interestingly, the three of us have landed on different structural models yet they have all stayed true to the original principles of filial including the primacy of the child-teacher relationship and the use of play sessions to build that relationship. Differences among our models typically include the length of the initial training, the ways in which play sessions are supervised, and the methods for transitioning play session skills into the classroom. Stulmaker (2013) provides a brief history and comparison of filial models used with teachers. Attachment B provides a summary of research conducted on filial models for teachers.

In Ray et al. (2004), we describe a brief model of implementing Relationship Enhancement for Learner and Teacher (RELATe) in which we lead a 1-day training, followed by live observations of weekly play sessions between students and teachers. In Carlson's (2013) study, we added a transitional phase following play sessions wherein the play therapist led and co-led three guidance sessions with the teacher to provide interactive modeling for skills in the classroom. In the more traditional Child-Teacher Relationship Training (Bennett & Helker, 2020), initial training is 2 days followed by 5 weekly supervision sessions of video-recorded sessions, then 10 weeks of classroom coaching for the teacher. Our teams conduct filial for teachers in both individual and groups formats. The group format allows for helpful relational support between teachers while the individual format allows for flexibility in scheduling. My take away from our experimentation is creativity and flexibility is key to implementation. Each school, grade level team, and individual teacher has unique needs which can be met when we are flexible with the model.

In the last 20 years, extensive research has demonstrated that filial interventions for teachers are effective in improving child disruptive behaviors in the classroom, externalizing and internalizing problem behaviors, student attendance, academic effort, and literacy (See Attachment B). On the teacher side, teachers who participate in filial interventions report better classroom management skills, greater satisfaction with their jobs, higher levels of empathy for their students, and improved student relationships. In schools where resources are limited and challenges are many, teachers who participated in filial training reported feeling more competence and less stress related to their roles as teachers (Post et al., 2020a). All of the teacher play-based interventions are built upon the foundations of filial therapy which proposes that adults who have everyday interaction with children can use the language of play and characteristics of a quality relationship to help children reach their full potential. Differences among the play-based interventions have mostly centered on the methods and delivery of training. For example, some models present training in group formats while others use individual formats. Some models involve weekly meetings while others are less intensive. Some content of training is different among the versions based on particular philosophical leanings toward counseling approaches. However, all filial teacher models are grounded in the following tenets:

1 The relationship between student and teacher is the primary agent of change for children.
2 The child's natural language of play is the primary communication tool.
3 The play session between child and teacher is the most favorable structure to build the relationship.
4 The child is capable of determining the most helpful content for play and is allowed to lead the play.
5 The teacher follows the child's lead.

6   The teacher learns and engages in specific verbal and non-verbal ways of communicating to facilitate the student-teacher relationship and the child's development.

7   Play times between students and teachers lead to moments of joy and connection that transfer to the classroom.

In years of conducting and researching the implementation of play therapy skills with teachers, we have learned information and skills that work in helping teachers develop more rewarding relationships with students, reduce behavioral problems in the classroom, improve teacher classroom management skills, and bring more joy to the role of being a teacher. PlayBreaks, the play times that are facilitated by teachers, harness the relational nature of play therapy to target building positive relationships with children that help children to function better in the classroom and within the student-teacher relationship. The experiences and information that teachers learn in PlayBreaks can guide them to develop healing relationships with children on individual and classroom levels.

7

The PlayBreak: A Special Playtime

The cornerstone of implementing best practices of play in schools is the Play-Break. The PlayBreak is an individual or small group playtime implemented by teachers to use the power of play and relationship to enhance their relationships with students and improve student attitudes and behaviors. The PlayBreak was developed using the lessons and information gathered from implementation of play therapy in the schools over the last 40 years. The purpose of PlayBreaks is to use what we know is most effective for children to help them build self-regulation, social skills, and contribute to holistic wellness and development: The relationship between student and teacher. PlayBreaks also have the added benefit of helping teachers capture the joy of being with their students. There are five goals for PlayBreaks:

1   Offer extra relational support to students in need
2   Improve relationships with most difficult students
3   Practice verbal and non-verbal skills for teachers to use in the classroom
4   Reduce instructional time lost to disciplinary problems
5   Enhance the joy of teaching

For PlayBreaks, the teacher will arrange a time to play with one or two children for a specific set amount of time. Ideally, the PlayBreak will be a 20–30 minute time period but may be shortened to meet schedule needs. PlayBreaks can often be effective if held for 10–15 minutes. For the PlayBreak, the teacher invites a child to a section of a classroom or another room within the school that can

DOI: 10.4324/9781003285618-10

serve as a playroom. The playroom is designed to include toys/materials organized in a specific arrangement. During the PlayBreak, the child determines the content of the play or conversation and the teacher follows the child's lead.

The PlayBreak Space

The PlayBreak space is a separate space from the classroom and is preferably in a room designated by the school as a playroom. Spaces such as converted conference rooms, testing rooms, book rooms, empty classrooms, and portable buildings are ideally suited for playrooms. The optimal dimensions for a playroom space is 12 × 15 feet (Landreth, 2012) but most playrooms are much smaller. In schools, it is common to mark off the space using book shelves or curtains hanging from ceilings. Although it is difficult to ensure a confidential space in a school setting, teachers should try to find spaces where the child can be comfortable playing without being observed by others. Confidential spaces allow for the child to feel at ease and engage in play that is less influenced by others. Essential features of a playroom include shelves for placing toys above the floor and allowing more room for free movement. Figures 7.1 and 7.2 depict two different playroom settings in schools.

Toys in a playroom are carefully and reflectively selected (Landreth, 2012). The purposes of toys and materials in a PlayBreak space are to allow children to express their thoughts and feelings about their worlds and experiences within their worlds. This expression optimally takes place in the context of a safe, trusting relationship. Therefore, toys and materials in the playroom are selected based on their potential to allow child expression and

Figure 7.1 School Playroom 1
Note: Shelves serve as the barrier between the play area and the rest of the classroom.

Figure 7.2 School Playroom 2
Note: The right wall of the playroom is marked off by curtains.

build relationship with the teacher. Due to the intentional selection of toys for these purposes, toys such as board games, technology-based materials, and traditional teaching materials (i.e., books) are not considered appropriate for a PlayBreak space. Materials such as board games and books are commonly used in only the ways intended with specific rules and often used to teach children specific skills or information. Technology-based materials such as video games have limited potential for developing authentic relationships, and again, typically are used in schools as teaching tools. Although these types of materials have a role in schools, materials in PlayBreaks are intended for the child to fully express themselves through symbolic and social play in the context of a healing relationship with the teacher. Hence, PlayBreak materials and toys are selected to meet these purposes.

In order for a child to develop trust in the playtime, consistent order and presentation of toys and materials is a key characteristic of a playroom. Toys are generally categorized by five general areas including family/nurturing, scary toys, expressive toys, pretend/fantasy toys, and aggressive toys (Kottman & Meany-Walen, 2016). For the family/nurturing category, materials provide the child the opportunity to act in the role of adult or child especially within family contexts. Materials include toys representative of items typically found in a home including kitchen and cleaning materials, as well as dolls. Scary toys include materials that are typically seen as fear-inducing such as snakes and spiders. In a playroom, scary toys allow children to express fears and anxieties they experience every day and may have gone unnoticed by adults. Expressive toys and materials include arts and crafts materials and allow for expression of creativity. Expressive materials, such as paints, craft and drawing materials, and sand, are used by children for multiple reasons including emotional regulation, soothing, and development of creativity. Pretend/fantasy toys such as dress up clothes, puppets, and medical kits allow children to explore adult roles and experiences in a safe environment.

The final category of aggressive toys tends to be the most controversial of the toys suggested for a playroom, especially in a school setting. Most children are attracted on some level to toys that represent aggression. The drive for humans to be aggressive has been noted throughout history and is a normal part of human existence. The inclusion of aggressive toys in a playroom is a message of acceptance to a child that all parts of them will be honored during PlayBreaks. The teacher's acknowledgment of a child's most basic human characteristic frees the child from being guilty and confused about these feelings. Through play with aggressive toys, children are allowed to explore their thoughts and feelings in a safe play environment so that they may sort out all the messages sent through the media and familial community about the role of aggression in getting their needs met in larger society. In several play therapy research studies, we have shown that when children have access to aggressive toys and play in a safe environment, they actually reduce their aggressive behaviors at home and school (Bratton et al., 2013; Ray et al., 2009; Schottelkorb et al., 2020; Wilson & Ray, 2018). In play therapy, aggressive toys include guns, knives, rope, and handcuffs, among other aggressive toys. However, in working with teachers over the years, I have observed that some teachers are very uncomfortable with some of these items and this discomfort impairs their ability to be fully present for the child during PlayBreaks. In these cases, a teacher may decide that some toys, such as a toy dart gun, may not be appropriate for the PlayBreak spaces; yet inclusion of some aggressive toys is essential to the play process for children.

In addition to the careful selection of toys in the given categories, teachers need to be intentional to ensure that their playrooms are culturally inclusive for the children in their classrooms. In a recent study on multicultural playrooms, play therapy experts encouraged therapists to intentionally structure playrooms and select materials that are

> accessible, diverse, and representative of many cultures, including but not limited to materials for categories of household, kitchen, food, dolls and figures, expressive materials, costumes, and transportation,

with particular attention to forms, textures and colors that are diverse
and representative of many cultures.

(Ray et al., 2022)

As teachers design their playrooms, they will want to include materials/toys
that are representative of the communities they serve. The following is a list
of materials recommended for PlayBreak spaces. This list is a condensed version of materials typically used in a play therapy room. The list was compiled
based on typical school setting limitations. If you are interested in setting up
a more comprehensive playroom, please refer to Landreth's (2012) *Play Therapy: The Art of the Relationship* (Table 7.1).

Table 7.1 *List of Toys/Materials for PlayBreaks*

Family/ Nurturing	Scary	Expressive	Pretend/Fantasy	Aggressive
Band-aids (various colors)	Snake	Building blocks	Hats: firefighter, police, tiara, crown	Bop bag
Doll family (small figures representative of community)	Spider	Crayons, pencils, paper, glue, tape, scissors	Medical kit	Dart gun
Small dollhouse	Scary puppet	Construction paper	Medical masks	Dinosaurs, shark
Kitchen dishes/ silverware		Drum	Play money	Handcuffs
Pots/pans		Sandbox with sand (consider a plastic bin if unable to have a sandbox)	Transportation vehicles (school bus, ambulance, car, airplane)	Rope
Baby bottle		Ball	Phones (2×)	Rubber knife
Baby doll (representative of community)			Zoo and farm animal families	Shield
			Puppets (aggressive and nurturing; 2–4×)	

In the PlayBreak space, toys and materials should be arranged by category and remain in the same place for each PlayBreak. This level of consistency instills a sense of trust in the space for the child. Figures 7.1 and 7.2 are pictures of how a PlayBreak space might be arranged.

Thus far, I have presented the structure and organization of a PlayBreak space when conditions are optimal and a teacher has access to separate space. Yet, there are many times where teachers are limited by their settings. Under these conditions, PlayBreaks can still occur when the teacher is creative. If a teacher is unable to identify a separate play space from their classroom, a portion of the classroom can be sectioned off to serve as a play space. Play spaces can be small and still be functional. I have set up spaces as small as 6 × 6 ft. Children love to play and they love that their teacher is willing and excited to play with them so they tend to not be critical of the space. Another common limitation is that teachers are unable to secure a stable play space that remains intact for each session. In this case, teachers can use a portable play kit such as a box or rolling cart. Portable play kits allow the teacher to hold PlayBreaks in various parts of the school with minimal set up. Figure 7.3 gives a picture of a portable play kit laid out for a session. You will notice that the blanket serves as a visual marker of the play space and toys are still laid out in an organized order. These types of modifications are common for PlayBreaks and allow for teachers to be versatile in facilitating the play times.

Figure 7.3 Portable PlayBreak Space

Traditional PlayBreak Schedule

The traditional PlayBreak schedule involves identification of a child of focus with whom you will hold a PlayBreak one time a week over 6 weeks for 20-minute play times. Teachers typically hold PlayBreaks during their planning periods, at lunch time, during specials (e.g., art, music, physical education), before or after school. Some classrooms have both teacher and paraprofessional teams which allows for the teacher or paraprofessional to hold Play-Breaks while the other team member remains in the classroom. For the child, it is best if the teacher does not choose times that interfere with activities that the child looks forward to, such as recess or a special that they particularly enjoy. The teacher is careful to hold PlayBreaks consistently with the child at the same time each week and is careful to maintain the time boundary. Just as the playroom sends a message of safety through consistency of organization and content, the structure of holding playtimes at a consistent time also establishes safety in the relationship. The traditional PlayBreak schedule is limited to six playtimes in order for the teacher to extend PlayBreaks to other children and to provide a practical timeline for school settings. However, if the teacher prefers to extend play sessions, there is no hard limit on the number of sessions.

Modified PlayBreak Schedule

Because schools are fluid environments and resources are scarce in many cases, a teacher's ability to offer six play sessions consistently over 6 weeks for 20 minutes each time may be limited. In these cases, there are modifications that can be made yet still provide the benefits of PlayBreaks. Session times may be limited to 15 minutes rather than 20. A teacher may decide to have two playtimes a week with a child for 3 weeks rather than extend over 6 weeks. The recommended six play times may be reduced to shorten the overall length of the intervention. All of these modifications are reasonable and my experience has shown that students and teachers still reap the benefits from PlayBreaks under these adjustments. Yet, with modifications there are still considerations that are recommended to stay in place including the focus on consistency. If playtimes are limited to 15 minutes, the teacher ensures that it is the entire 15 minutes each time. If playtimes are twice a week, the teacher has a schedule for the same 2 days and times each week. If there will be less than six playtimes, the teacher has informed the child of the number prior to starting PlayBreaks rather than stating there will be six and then reducing to less. Although it might be necessary to reduce PlayBreak sessions, benefits are limited when less than six sessions are held.

Identification of Students of Focus

The initiation of PlayBreaks starts with selecting a child of focus. The term "child of focus" is an intentional term used to convey the attitude of relationship that contextualizes PlayBreaks. The child of focus is a child who the teacher believes can benefit from having a relationship in which the child experiences full presence and acceptance. Although teachers often select children who exhibit disruptive behaviors, the child of focus is not conceptualized as a "problem child" or "child with a behavioral issue" but as a child who is struggling with the everyday challenges of school. The child of focus is typically a child with whom the teacher is also struggling relationally as manifested through disciplinary issues, compassion limitations, or alternately, excessive sympathy. In order to choose a child of focus, the following exercise may help in your decision-making.

Close your eyes and picture your classroom. As you picture your classroom, visualize each child as you go around the room, making sure that you see each child individually in your mind. Take a moment to take in each child. After you've seen each child, go back to one of the children who you feel most emotional about. Picture that child. Picture yourself with that child. What are your feelings that come up when you picture this child? How strong are you feeling? How would you describe this child? How would you describe yourself when you think about this child? How would you describe yourself when you interact with this child? When you open your eyes, write down your answers to these questions.

As you look at your answers, you will want to weigh the possible benefits and challenges to selecting this child as your child of focus. PlayBreaks are meant for the children that bring up the most emotional responses in teachers. However, there are drawbacks to starting with a child for whom you have stronger emotional responses. On one hand, selecting this child is likely to bring you greater empathy and understanding of this child so that your classroom interaction can be more successful. On the other hand, if you are just starting PlayBreaks, this child might be a bigger challenge than you expected for a new type of intervention. You may consider starting PlayBreaks with a child who brings up less emotion in you and who you want to get to know better. However, the goal would be to eventually offer PlayBreaks to the children with whom you struggle the most. PlayBreaks are beneficial for all children but they are especially effective in building and repairing relationships between teachers and children with emotional and behavioral challenges.

8

The PlayBreak Attitudes

The space has been defined, the materials selected, the time structure organized, and a child of focus identified. These structural elements are essential to the success of PlayBreaks. Yet, the most attention in PlayBreaks should be paid to the relational environment set by the teacher. After all, the relationship is the healing agent of change for PlayBreaks. The teacher's attitudes and skills facilitate the play relationship toward greater understanding and acceptance of the child while also providing a foundation for the child to reach their full potential.

Entering the PlayBreak Space

In learning to be a teacher, we are typically taught how to organize a lesson plan, how to measure learning, and possibly, classroom management. What we are typically not taught is how to build relationships with students that lead to greater learning outcomes. Many teachers are naturally gifted with interpersonal skills and are adept at building relationships in the classroom. Yet, even the most relationally strong teachers need attitudes, skills, and tools in place to intentionally build relationships with students. There are five particular teacher attitudes that underlie the success of a PlayBreak: (a) valuing and respecting play as the natural language of communication and expression for children; (b) operating from a place of genuineness and authenticity; (c) seeking to have full acceptance and prizing of a child; (d) striving for

DOI: 10.4324/9781003285618-11

empathic understanding of a child; and (e) holding a multicultural orientation (MCO) toward each child.

Valuing and Respecting Play

The early part of this book laid out the benefits of play for child development and how play contributes to learning outcomes. PlayBreaks are built upon the knowledge that play is the way that children most naturally express their worlds, learn to regulate their emotions and behaviors, and build social skills. Often in the adult culture, play is viewed as a luxury, a privilege, or a reward. The school culture has been especially drawn into the cultural view that play should be used as a reward, rather than valuing play as essential to development. As a result, limiting recess is often used as a disciplinary measure or free center time is used as a reward for good behavior. The teacher who uses PlayBreaks will hold an attitude of respect for the activity of play as fundamental to understanding of and communicating with children. The PlayBreak teacher acknowledges that the child is most likely to communicate their emotions and confusion through play and is most likely to develop regulatory and coping skills through play. Children use symbolic play to organize and understand their worlds more fully, as well as use play to show their worlds to others. Children also use social play to build their interpersonal skills and relationships. They use their play in much deeper ways than they use their newly acquired verbal language skills which are often inadequate for expressing their most complicated inner thoughts and feelings. In Play-Breaks, the teacher moves into the child's developmental world of play rather than insist that the child move into the adult world of verbal language.

Genuineness and Authenticity

When I was educated as teacher, I quickly learned from observing my senior teachers and mentors that genuineness was not valued as a quality of a strong teacher. In fact, genuineness related to any type of vulnerability such as not feeling competent, getting my feelings hurt by a student, or being overwhelmed was considered a weakness in a teacher. "Good teachers" have it together, always win the power struggles, and don't let the little things get them down. I have seen this attitude in teachers remain consistent over the last 30 years and I believe this attitude interferes with building effective learning relationships with students, not to mention interfering with building effective support networks. Although teachers should strive to be emotionally regulated and behaviorally consistent in the classroom, children appreciate teachers and adults who authentically present themselves. The first step toward becoming more genuine in the classroom is to recognize and accept all parts of ourselves as humans. Being able to recognize the stronger and weaker qualities helps us to learn to accept these parts of ourselves. If I deny parts of myself, such as being too controlling or doubting myself too much, those parts will tend to sneak up on me, leading me to operate from them without awareness. Behaviors without awareness can lead to more destructive outcomes. Yet, if I allow myself to see that sometimes I can be too controlling and those times are linked to when I am challenged by another person, then I can start to change those behaviors without criticizing myself for having that tendency. Or I might struggle with a great need to be liked by others. When I am unaware of this need, I will operate with overly pleasing behaviors that lead to allowing children to cross boundaries in the classroom. Yet, again, if I allow myself to accept this part of myself, I am more aware when I am motivated by this need and act more consciously with the awareness. One of the key limitations to becoming more genuine is not allowing yourself to own all parts of who you are, the good, the bad, and the in-between.

Once a teacher has fully accepted all parts of the self, genuineness involves decisions regarding transparency. If I am feeling overwhelmed with all the things happening in the classroom in the moment, do I sit down and cry or possibly scream or walk out? Those would certainly all be genuine responses but not exactly helpful to the children or the teacher's relationship to the children. However, a calm and regulated response in which the teacher shares "I am feeling overwhelmed by all the different things happening in here so I'm choosing to lower the lights and hold one minute of silence" is one way to demonstrate genuineness and appropriate transparency. The PlayBreak teacher values this type of genuineness and transparency. There are times in PlayBreaks when a teacher may feel uncertain or lacking in confidence. Instead of putting on a disingenuous face of "I got this," the teacher responds with "I'm not sure," "I don't know," "Seems like I should know that but I don't." These types of genuine responses allow a child to experience the teacher as vulnerable and more like them which sets the stage for the child to be fully vulnerable and expressive in PlayBreaks. When a child experiences a teacher as genuine, they are more likely to experience the teacher as someone who can be trusted.

Full Acceptance and Prizing of the Child

The attitude that is arguably the most effective attitude in facilitating growth and development for a child is the concept described by Rogers (1957) as unconditional positive regard. The concept of unconditional positive regard has been around in the counseling and play therapy world for a long time. Unconditional positive regard has several characteristics including acceptance and prizing of the child and belief in the capability of the child. Rogers (1969) even talked about prizing the student as an "imperfect human being with many feelings, many potentialities" (p. 109). Acceptance of the child is accepting the child just as they are, not wishing they were different in some way (Axline, 1947). This particular concept is often misunderstood in educational settings and may be misinterpreted as allowing a child to *do* whatever they want. Yet, that is not the principle being highlighted. Acceptance of a child means that I accept and prize the person of the child. I do not wish that the child were fundamentally different, such as wishing they were more like another (e.g., nicer, organized, calmer). The irony is that when we fully accept children as they are, in that moment is when they are free to change (Rogers, 1961). It is when we insist that children be different than who they are (less of this and more of that) that we see them more rigidly hold on to their behaviors which may be destructive but are comfortable and comforting to them. When we accept them as they are, they feel less pressure to change by others and will likely free their internal worlds to experiment with what it is like to be or act differently. Along with this acceptance of the person of the child, the teacher also prizes the child as a valued and worthy person. The child is a person with whom the teacher wants to spend time and is honored to do so. This type of genuine prizing of a child is an antidote to all the negative messages sent to children on a daily basis, especially those children who struggle in school.

The other key characteristic of unconditional positive regard is the teacher's belief in the capability of the child. In a school setting, teachers are often taught and enculturated that children only thrive through guidance and direct teaching. Some schools hold little value in students' abilities to make decisions about what is best for them. In PlayBreaks, teachers believe and demonstrate the belief that the child is capable of leading and directing their own play. Tapping into the concept that children have an internal locus of control that can be trusted to lead them toward self and other-enhancement, PlayBreak teachers trust that the child will use playtimes to express and communicate what is of most value to the child. Although teachers have various and substantial roles in teaching and guiding students, the structure of Play-Breaks allows teachers to be able to live out their belief in children's capabilities and observe what happens when children are able to choose their paths in play. Unconditional positive regard is an attitude that can be challenging for teachers and school systems because adults can often see children heading in what appears to be the wrong direction and feel compelled to alter their course. PlayBreaks allow children to experiment with decision-making through integrating their desires with their behaviors in a structured yet safe environment. In this PlayBreak environment, the teacher can facilitate the child's methods of building coping skills and dealing with consequences without intervening with correction or direct guidance, thereby seeing the child make great strides toward mature functioning.

Empathic Understanding

During PlayBreaks, we ask teachers to seek empathic understanding of the child. Empathic understanding, often referred to as empathy, is the ability of the teacher to see the world as the child sees the world. In other words, the teacher seeks to understand the child's feelings, thoughts, and perceptions about the world based on the child's worldview. During play, children will open up their worlds and show how their coping skills have developed based on their experiences. The teacher's role is to develop a greater understanding of how the child has made sense of their world and how the child has established ways of being in the world based on that meaning. Through empathic understanding, the teacher is able to deepen their compassion for the child and communicate this care back to the child. When the child is able to perceive empathy from the teacher, they know they are not alone. The child knows that there is another person who can really understand them and cares about them.

In schools, we talk quite a bit about empathy and teaching children how to build empathy toward others. There are a great many curriculums dedicated to teaching children how to be empathic. Yet, we have learned through child development research that children develop empathy by receiving empathy. For most children, this experience comes from their primary caregivers during infancy. However, many of the children with most challenging behavioral concerns did not receive these empathic experiences in the younger years and can only draw from an empty well. Shamay-Tsoory (2011) identified two types of empathy from a neural perspective that are dependent on different parts of the brain: cognitive and affective empathy. Cognitive empathy is a process that takes place through the prefrontal cortex using thought processes that result in being able to identify and think of another's feelings. Whereas, affective empathy takes place through the limbic system (e.g., insula, amygdala, and ACC) and results in being able to feel another's feelings. Based on these brain structures, it is most likely that affective empathy is a direct result of experiences which are encoded in the brain and therefore are dependent on receiving empathy. From the PlayBreak perspective, the most effective way for children to learn empathy is not through teaching but through providing ongoing experiences of empathy. During PlayBreaks, teachers provide these types of empathic experiences to children who ideally are able to perceive the feeling of empathy and create new neural networks connecting relational experiences with positive feelings and expectations. For those children who did not receive these empathic interactions in their early years, this type of teacher-provided intervention can literally change the emotional brain of children.

A word about acceptance and empathy. The combination of full acceptance and empathic experiencing during PlayBreak interactions is a powerful antidote to the negative experiences of childhood. Acceptance and empathy work in tandem to send the message to the child that

> I understand how the world looks to you and why you choose to operate in the world the way you do. I deeply care about you and your feelings about your world. And I honor your worthiness and unique way of being.

When a child is able to experience these attitudes from their teacher, they feel empowered and encouraged to reach their full potential.

Multicultural orientation. School systems are grounded in specific cultural values and practices. Typically, schools are hierarchically structured and work from a top-down approach whereby there is a central administrative figure, a small number of middle administrative figures, teachers, paraprofessionals, and then students. The hierarchy is well-maintained with disciplinary practices emanating from the top person with the most power and delivered to the bottom group, students who have the least amount of power. The hierarchical and patriarchal structure of schools has been identified as contributory to systemic oppression that maintains dominant cultural values. Within school systems are the schools themselves. Each school develops its own culture that may or may not represent its community and develops practices in working with the diversity of students within the school. Again, it is common for a local school to be attuned to the dominant culture of the community and to miss or actively resist diverse cultural perspectives of minority students. Cultural values play a large role in the systems within schools and also on the individual level. Each individual teacher and individual student within a school identifies with myriad of cultural identities and practices. From an individual perspective, schools serve as a fishbowl of unique, intersecting, and common cultural values among individuals and small groups of individuals.

In order to fully enact the attitudes of genuineness, acceptance, and empathic understanding, a teacher embraces an attitude of seeking cultural understanding and inclusion. The MCO framework as presented in Owen et al. (2011) and further examined in Davis et al. (2018) is guided by a philosophy of the importance of cultural factors (e.g., racial/ethnic identity, gender, religious affiliation) in our work with others. Within the MCO, cultural humility, cultural opportunities, and cultural comfort act as the three pillars of the orientation. *Cultural humility* indicates that the teacher holds an attitude of humility and a focus on the other rather than the self. When holding an attitude of cultural humility, the teacher recognizes that there are a multiplicity of truths and experiences based on a person's identities, background, and experiences (Davis et al., 2018). In PlayBreaks, cultural humility is demonstrated through the teacher's desire to see the full world of the child and how their cultural beliefs and experiences are manifested in their worldview. Cultural humility encourages the teacher to suspend judgment regarding the child's experiences and seek to value the child's intersecting cultural identities. When a teacher engages in cultural humility, they are more likely to recognize *cultural opportunities* from which the teacher can actively enter into exploration of the child's cultural identity and experiences. Also, through cultural humility, the teacher will experience a greater level of *cultural comfort* indicating that the teacher is able to enter into conversations or play with a greater sense of ease and genuineness. When a teacher can value and engage in an MCO, a student is likely to feel better understood, more fully known, which deepens the relationship between the teacher and child. After all, being truly authentic, accepting of others, and striving to see another's worldview are qualities of an MCO.

The teacher's ability to experience and communicate the relational attitudes is the core of the PlayBreak and remains the most essential quality of teacher-student interaction. The PlayBreak teacher will almost assuredly be working on attitudes consistently over the course of play times, daily student interaction, and throughout the year. Attitudes exist on a continuum rather than on a dichotomy of existence. Teachers will strive at different points on the continuum with individual students and with individual situations. There is no perfection when it comes to teacher attitudes. The goal is to continue to endeavor toward holding the attitudes and seeking to be humanly authentic while doing so.

9

The PlayBreak Skills

As teachers strive toward reaching and sustaining relational attitudes, Play-Breaks involve the use of skills that help to demonstrate these attitudes. Skills are divided into two categories of non-verbal skills and verbal skills. Non-verbal skills are ways of being in the playroom that send a message of presence, acceptance, and authenticity. The seven verbal skills are utilized by teachers during play times to help facilitate the child's play and the teacher-student relationship. They include tracking, reflection of content, reflection of feelings, encouragement, returning responsibility, facilitating creativity, facilitating relationship, and limit-setting.

Non-Verbal Skills

During PlayBreaks, the teacher follows the child's lead in play and conversation. There are a few guidelines that help structure the play times so that teachers are in a follower role. First, the teacher does not name or label toys before the child does. In a child's play, a toy or material can be whatever they want it to be. A monkey can be a mother, a paintbrush can be a sword, or a ball can be the sun. When a teacher labels the toy, the child is limited in their imagination and their potential creativity with that toy. By not labeling toys, the child is free to imagine the toy as whatever is needed for the child to play out their intended scenes. Because teachers do not label toys until the child does, it is common to use words like "this" or "that" when

DOI: 10.4324/9781003285618-12

initially referring to toys. For example, a teacher might say, "You really like playing with that one," or "You wanted this one the most." Once a child has named a toy, the teacher is free to follow the child's lead in referring to the toys as labeled. However, the teacher remains flexible in following the child because the child might quickly decide to label one toy with multiple names.

The teacher only enters the play when requested by the child. In a Play-Break playroom, the teacher has a designated spot for sitting which can be in a chair or on the floor with some distance between the teacher and child. The distance serves to send the message to the child that this space is theirs, not the teacher's. The teacher is emotionally present with the child but allows some space so that the teacher does not intrude into the child's play unless invited. The child will decide when they desire to play with the teacher or feel safe enough for the teacher to come closer or come further into their space. Because of immense external pressures in the outside world and the alternate safe place offered by PlayBreaks, some children will use PlayBreaks to play quietly without involving the teacher. These types of PlayBreaks can serve to facilitate calmness and regulation for children and it is a powerful relational message that a teacher still wants to be in the playtime with a child even when the child is not entertaining the teacher.

The teacher remains physically open to the child during the PlayBreak. Typically, the teacher will sit with arms and legs uncrossed in an open position and leaned toward the child. The physical openness toward the child sends the message of emotional availability and interest in the child. As the child moves, the teacher will physically orient themselves toward the child. Moving physically in the direction of the child is called the "toes follow nose" technique (Landreth, 2012); in that, if the teacher moves their head to face the child, their whole body should follow.

The teacher's tone of voice is another non-verbal way of sending a message of care and presence to the child, as well as genuineness. In verbally responding to the child, the teacher attempts to match the child's tone. If the child is angry, the teacher responds in a lower tone, rather than an overly animated happy tone that is often used to try to distract or make the child feel better. If the child is excited, the teacher matches that tone with a lighter voice. The matching of tone sends a message that the child is allowed to express any emotion and it is valued by the teacher. In addition to matching the child's tone, the teacher should also attempt to authentically match their words with their own tone. For example, if a teacher is setting a limit with a child but uses a happy, lighter tone, the child experiences this interaction as disingenuous which may limit the child's trust in the teacher.

Verbal Skills

Verbal skills are the actual verbal responses used by teachers during Play-Breaks. Initially, verbal skills are difficult to master because they represent a very different style of communicating than typically used by adults with children. The seven verbal skills are designed to allow a child to lead and to facilitate specific areas of growth for children. Just as there were guidelines for non-verbal skills, there are several guidelines that help structure verbal skills. First, a teacher is careful to use short sentences and phrases in all verbal responses. Typically, verbal responses are less than ten words (Landreth, 2012). When adults use more words than needed, children often lose focus, miss the meaning of what is being said, or feel compelled to make the adult the center of attention. Brief responses allow the child to continue in play and conversation while encouraging interaction.

Consistent with the goal of allowing the child to lead, teachers do not ask questions during PlayBreaks. Questions are motivated by the adult's agenda, not the child's. When a teacher asks a question of a child, the child feels required to respond on the adult's terms in the adult's language. Such an interaction places the teacher in the lead and the child as the follower. The goals of PlayBreaks are met through the child's lead; hence, the teacher avoids leading the conversation or play through questioning the child. Finally, most verbal responses should be personalized by starting with the word "you." Starting responses with "you" indicates that the PlayBreak is about the child and that the teacher is genuinely interested in the child. These guidelines underpin the seven categories of verbal responses. The following section defines the seven skills in more detail and Table 9.1 provides a succinct explanation and example for each skill.

Table 9.1 *Verbal Responses for PlayBreak and the Classroom*

Response Category	Target Factor	Description
Tracking behavior	Set tone for relationship – sending message child is in lead	Teacher verbally responds to behavior of the child by stating what is observed. *"You're picking that up."*
Reflecting content	Build empathy Model social skills Develop self-concept	Teacher paraphrases the verbal interaction of the child. *"You went to see the pirate movie and there was a lot of fighting in it."*

(Continued)

Response Category	Target Factor	Description
Reflecting feeling	Build empathy Model social skills Develop self-concept	Teacher verbally responds to emotions expressed by child. *"You're angry about the glue bottle not working."*
Returning responsibility	Increase emotional regulation Improve decision-making Increase sense of capability Build self-responsibility	Teacher verbalizes statements to help children experience their own capability and take responsibility for it. *"You decided you would be the boss and take charge."* *"That looks like something you can do."*
Facilitating creativity	Encourage emotional expression Expand coping skills	Teacher verbalizes statements that help a child experience a sense of freedom and creativity. *"In here, it can be whatever you want it be."*
Esteem-building/ Encouragement	Develop self-concept Increase sense of capability	Teacher verbalizes statements to help children experience a stronger and capable sense of self. *"You did it. You tried hard and figured it out."*
Facilitating relationship	Build empathy Deepen relationship	Teacher reflects statements that build the relationship between teacher and child. *"You wanted to be close to me."* *"You wanted to make dinner for me."*
Limit-setting	Increase emotional regulation Improve decision-making Build self-responsibility	Limits are set according to a 3-step procedure of reflecting the child's intention of feeling, setting a definitive limit, and providing an appropriate alternative. *"You are frustrated with the sword but the sword is not for breaking. You can tear the paper."*

Tracking

Tracking is the starting point for the PlayBreak and for the relationship. Tracking is following the lead of the child in their play through verbal responses. When tracking, the teacher will simply state what the child is doing at the time. When a child picks up a doll, the teacher might use a tracking response like, "You're picking that up," or when a child moves across the room to look at a toy, the teacher may say "You're going to check that out." Through tracking, the teacher sends the message immediately that this is a time where the child is the focus and that the teacher is authentically interested in the child. Tracking also allows a teacher the ability to make responses even when a child is non-verbal or teacher is unclear about the child's play. Tracking is a response that is usually new for most teachers and it takes a while to feel comfortable tracking in a relaxed manner. Initially, teachers may track too frequently or too infrequently but once they practice, it becomes a much easier skill and tracking helps teachers become more present in the room and with the child.

Reflection of Content and Feelings

Reflective listening and observation is a basic skill for meaningful interactions between people and this is no different for PlayBreaks. During PlayBreaks, teachers seek to listen to a child's talk and observe the child at play. In deep listening and observation, the teacher then reflects back what they have heard or seen in the form of reflections of content or reflections of feelings. Reflection of content involves reflecting back to the child what they have shared through conversation with the teacher. For example, if a child shares that they went to see a movie with their family on Saturday and the movie was really long and they got to get a large popcorn, the teacher may use a reflection of content by saying, "You got to go with your family to the movie and you got a special treat too." When reflecting content, the teacher is showing that they were listening carefully and they understood what the child was telling them. This type of reflective listening sends the message to the child that what they say is important and valued by the teacher. This message of worthiness works toward increasing a child's self-esteem and builds relationships skills. Reflecting feeling is the expression of empathic understanding from teacher to child. When the child perceives empathy, the expectation is that the child will build a greater capacity for sharing empathy for others.

Reflection of feeling is a deeper level of reflective listening because it moves beyond reflecting only content of a child's sharing and more into the internal experience of the child. When reflecting feeling, a teacher is listening to the words, tone, and facial/physical expressions of the child, then reflecting back the feeling communicated by the child. Sometimes the child will directly share their feelings while at other times, the teacher is only using non-verbal cues to identify the child's feelings. For example, in an angry voice when trying to open a bottle of glue, a child says, "I hate this stupid glue." The teacher may respond with a reflection of feeling, "You are really frustrated with that." Another example, a child sings happily as she is painting. The teacher may respond with "You are happy when you paint." Through reflecting feelings, the teacher again is building self-esteem and relationship skills; and in addition, the teacher is helping the child to feel heard and seen in a deeper way which helps with self-regulation and self-acceptance. A feelings list and practice exercises to improve your feeling reflections are included at the end of this chapter.

Encouragement/Self-Esteem Building

Throughout the PlayBreak, the teacher seeks opportunities to send messages of encouragement in order to build a child's self-esteem. Encouragement responses are used to notice the efforts of children rather than the accomplishments of children (Nelsen et al., 2013). Teachers can give encouraging statements to children in almost any situation if the teacher is observing closely. When a child is focusing on a certain kind of play, the teacher can respond with a statement such as, "you're working really hard on that" or "you're really focused on that."

Encouragement speaks to the intent and intrinsic motivation of a child. It is important to distinguish encouragement from praise. One of the goals of PlayBreaks is to facilitate a child's internal locus of control. In other words, we hope that children will start to make healthy decisions for themselves and others based on their own internal motivations rather than being pulled and pushed by external expectations and rewards or avoidance of punishment. Many teachers are taught to praise in order to increase a child's self-esteem yet praise can be problematic in the building of a child's internal locus of control for several reasons. Typically, praise is given as a holistic evaluation of the child such as, "you were so good today," "you're nice to your friends," or "you do great work." These broad generalizations are typically internalized by the child as evaluations of the self as a whole, such as "I am good or I am bad," "I am nice or I am mean," "my work is great or it is terrible." When this type of praise is given, the child becomes dependent upon external sources (i.e., parents, teachers) to evaluate themselves as a whole (e.g., I am good or I am bad) and their relationships (e.g., she likes me or she does not like me). When children are praised holistically, they learn to depend on these responses to evaluate themselves. As dependence grows on external sources of approval, internal sources of evaluation will begin to wane. Instead of a child stopping to think, "is this my best work or is this the way I want to be acting?," the child will learn to look outside themselves for constant reinforcers to tell them whether they are okay or not. The problem with this type of dependence is that we know as a person ages, there are less and less external reinforcers that lead to wellness and good decision-making. Ultimately, we hope that children will check internally to evaluate if their ways of thinking and behaving are helping themselves and others. A final problem with praise is that it is often provided with a manipulative intent by adults. Historically, teachers have been taught to use praise as a classroom management technique, such as "I see that Julie already has her book out and is ready to listen." In this type of praise, Julie is used as an object to shape other students' behaviors. Again, the mechanism of external evaluation is in effect so that from this interaction, students learn that they should do what Julie does in order for the teacher to be happy with them. And a side effect of this type of praise is the depersonalizing way that Julie is used sends the message to Julie that her worth is in modeling for others and doing what the teacher likes rather than being proud that she is organized and ready to go.

Whereas praise leads to external dependence, encouragement leads to internalized motivation for decision-making. As a child's self-concept is strengthened, they are more likely to engage in reflective decision-making grounded in an intrinsic evaluation. "I am a worthy and valued person. Is this behavior good for me? Will this behavior help in my relationships with others?" Another bonus of encouragement is that you can give it anytime. You do not have to wait for a child to accomplish something. Encouraging phrases, such as "you worked hard on that," "you kept trying," "you are really thinking about how to do that," are ways to build self-esteem even when the child is unsuccessful in their attempts. When a child does accomplish a task, responses such as "You did it!," "You kept working until you got it like you wanted it," "You're really proud of how you did that," or "You tried hard and you figured it out," let the child know you saw what is important to them and how hard they work. These types of phrases send the message that you really see the child, and not just the products or external presentation of the child. These are the types of messages that build self-concept. Table 9.2 provides a list of esteem-building statements that can be used in PlayBreaks and more broadly in the classroom.

Returning Responsibility

Returning responsibility responses are a truly unique aspect of PlayBreaks. The purpose of returning responsibility to children during play is to send a message of capability and build self-reflection on decision-making and consequences. In order to provide an attitude of unconditional positive regard

Table 9.2 *Encouragement Phrases for the PlayBreak and the Classroom*

You did it!	You figured it out!	You keep trying even when it's hard!
It's tough but you're not giving up!	You're proud of what you did!	You're figuring it out!
You're trying hard!	You just keep working hard!	That was a hard one but you did it!
You're trying again!	You're sticking with it!	You figured out a whole other way to do that!
You want to make sure you're doing your best!	You're not sure if you can do it, but you're going to take a chance!	You're going to try even if it's new to you!
You're really thinking hard about that!	You are using all your focus to do that!	That was hard but you stuck with it!
And now you're trying another way to do that!	You're really proud of yourself!	You like to figure things out!
You're choosing to try again!	You want to keep going until you figure it out!	That didn't work but you're trying again!
You are determined to figure this out!	You are really thinking about how to do that!	

that was discussed earlier in this chapter, the teacher seeks to communicate a belief in the child's ability to solve problems and engage in productive decision-making. Returning responsibility responses are used by the teacher to facilitate the child's lead in the PlayBreaks. When a child asks, "What should I do?" or "How do I play with this?," the teacher returns responsibility by saying, "In here, it's up to you" or "You can decide." This lets the child know that the PlayBreak time is a time that they will be engaged in leading and creating what they need to happen during the play. The child also receives the relational message from the teacher that they can be trusted to make decisions and to lead. Returning responsibility responses also highlight the child's decision-making abilities with sentence starters, such as "You decided...," "You're choosing...," "you have a plan..." If a child shows two elephants playing with each other and one says, "I like you" to the other one, the teacher might respond with "You decided those two would be friends." If a child picks up a ball to throw at the teacher but then changes his mind and throws it toward the door, the teacher might say, "You chose to throw it away from me." As a child concentrates on building a wall, the teacher might say, "Looks like you have a plan in mind." These types of responses send the message to the child that they have the ability to make different decisions and that they are responsible for those decisions. As a child decreases their dependence on others making decisions or creating consequences for them, they start to build their own decision-making capacities to make better decisions. Stronger abilities to make decisions help students engage their cognitive abilities with more consistency leading to self-regulation.

Facilitating Creativity/Spontaneity

As children build self-esteem and learn to engage in internally motivated decision-making, creativity will need to be facilitated. Creativity in children's play allows for multiple avenues of expression including drawing, painting, storytelling, building, and role-playing. In PlayBreaks, we facilitate creativity so that children can use all forms of expression and operate from a place of spontaneity and fun. Teachers facilitate creativity by allowing a child to lead the play and by responses such as, "In here, that can be whatever you want it to be" or "that's up to you." The playroom is a place where the child can experiment with many ideas and does not have to be constricted by previous ways of doing things or another person's opinion of what should be done. When children feel the freedom to be creative, one of the most exciting outcomes is that they will start to problem-solve using multiple ideas. Hence, another benefit of creativity for children in PlayBreaks is the development of creative ideas and solutions to deal with issues or obstacles. For example, if a child plays with two monkeys who are designated as mother and child wherein the mother becomes angry because the child monkey is screaming, the child may start to change the scene to have the child monkey change behaviors so the mother does not become angry. In this type of scenario, the child is trying out coping skills, using their own creativity to experiment with different ideas. When a child experiences freedom to unleash creativity, they become effective in problem-solving, leading to expansion of coping skills. There is often overlap between facilitating creativity and returning responsibility responses. When a teacher responds, "In here, that's up to you," the message is sent that the child's creativity is encouraged *and* decisions are the responsibility of the child.

Facilitating Relationship

The relationship between the teacher and the child is the heart of PlayBreaks which means that teacher responses should highlight the relationship whenever possible. Facilitating relationship responses directly address the relationship between teacher and child by using both words, "you" and "me." The teacher makes facilitating relationship responses when they notice the child is checking in, wanting something from the teacher, or wanting to give something to the teacher. The following are some examples of facilitating relationship responses. (1) A child tells the teacher that the teacher is sick and he is going to make soup for her. Teacher response: "You want to take care of me." (2) The child lifts the paint brush toward the wall and looks at the teacher but does not paint the wall. Teacher response: "You're looking at me. You're wondering what I think about you doing that." (3) The child accidentally spills glue on the floor and looks at the teacher worriedly. Teacher response: "You're really worried about me and what I think about that." (4) The child is excited to tell the teacher about her trip to see her grandmother. Teacher response, "You're so excited and you wanted to share all about it with me." All of these responses are targeted at responding to the child's valuing of the teacher and the relationship. They are intended to send the message that the teacher also values the relationship and is there to journey with the child in their play.

Limit-Setting

In relationships, boundaries are an essential feature. Setting boundaries helps to establish consistency and safety within a relationship so that each person develops a sense of trust in self and others. In PlayBreaks, the establishment of boundaries is called limit-setting. Limit-setting is a verbal response by the teacher to set the boundaries of the room and the relationship. As emphasized throughout this book, PlayBreaks are characterized by allowing permissiveness for a child's self-expression and creativity. However, there will be times that children engage in behaviors that may be harmful or lead to harm. Consistent with the philosophy that PlayBreaks thrive in a permissive environment, limits are only set as needed. Teachers do not set limits until the time that children actually initiate problem behaviors. Teachers state limits when a child attempts to hurt themselves or others or is destructive to materials or the room. Some behaviors that prompt limit-setting are unintentional such as a child becoming excited about painting and thinking it is fun to watch the paint spill on the floor. Other behaviors are more intentionally targeted at breaking typical rules such as throwing a ball at a window to see if it will break. Whether intentional or unintentional, the teacher will need to set limits on these types of behaviors. The goal of limit-setting is to help a child learn to accept responsibility for behaviors, understand consequences, regulate their emotions, and engage in more productive decision-making.

Setting limits the PlayBreak way is a very different skill than most teachers have been taught on their road to becoming a teacher. The limit-setting process involves three steps referred to as ACT which include

(A) Acknowledging the feeling, (C) Communicating the limit, and (T) Targeting an alternative (Landreth, 2012). Acknowledging the feeling or intention of the child is the first and priority step of the limit-setting process. When a teacher acknowledges the child's feelings or intention, this is the same skill as reflecting feeling. Just as the purpose of reflecting feeling is to send the message the teacher understands the child and cares about the child's feelings and desires, acknowledging feeling as the first of the limit-setting process allows the child to feel heard and understood. Acknowledging feeling initiates the self-regulation process by gaining the child's attention that the teacher cares about the child. Examples of acknowledging feelings might be, "You are excited about that paint," while acknowledging intentions/desires might be, "You want to see if you're strong enough to break that window."

The second step of ACT is communicating the limit. When the teacher sets the limit, the statement is a clear and direct limit on the behavior. The unique part of communicating the limit is that the teacher does not use "I" or "you" statements. Limits are stated as behaviors that are not for doing, such as "the paint is not for throwing," or "the window is not for breaking." I like to refer to limits as just rules of the universe of which I am the messenger. Limits simply exist and I am there to let the child know. Because the goal is for the child to learn to self-regulate and to make better decisions, we deliver limits in a way that allow the child to think and act in response to knowing the limits around them.

Here is an exercise that might help in seeing the importance of how we deliver limits. Imagine that you are a child that is trying to break a window by throwing a ball as hard as you can. The teacher says to you, "You can't throw the ball." What is your immediate reaction? Feeling? Most children (and most adults) have an immediate defiant reaction such as "sure I can, watch me" or "what are you going to do about it?" Now imagine the teacher says, "The ball is not for throwing at the window." What's your reaction to this statement? Maybe more of "Why not?" or "I really want to." This type of reaction slows down the child to start to think about what they are doing and deliberate on consequences rather than placing them in a reactive defiant power struggle against the person of the teacher.

The third step of ACT is to target an alternative behavior for the child. Often, children are acting impulsively during these times and have difficulty slowing down to engage in more purposeful decision-making. This dynamic is especially true for young children. Stating a different behavior that matches a child's need or feeling helps the child to redirect their energy into an appropriate behavior. Examples of targeting an alternative might be "you can paint the paper" or "you can throw the ball hard on the ground." Targeting an alternative also helps children see that there are other ways they can get their needs met and models creative decision-making for them.

When put all together, the ACT limit-setting process offers a method to establish boundaries while also fostering self-esteem, regulation, relationship, self-responsibility, decision-making, and coping skills. Using our prior examples, we can see how the process works in one quick statement. Example 1: "You are excited about the paint but the paint is not for throwing. You can paint the paper." Example 2: "You want to see if you're strong enough to break that window but the ball is not for throwing at the window. You can throw the ball hard on the ground." The handout at the end of this chapter can help as a reminder of the ACT structure, purposes, and examples.

The importance of how teachers deliver limit-setting cannot be over-emphasized enough. Tone of voice will make or break the success of limit-setting. Voice tones that sound authoritarian, annoyed, sarcastic, or meant to establish the teacher's power will often fail to reach the goal of facilitating a child's constructive decision-making abilities. These types of tones typically initiate a reactionary behavior or verbalization from the child, which takes them offline from their cognitive decision-making center. The ACT limit-setting method is unique because it is a way to establish limits that enable the child to reach loftier goals of responsibility, regulation, and coping skills, rather than just stopping an immediate behavior (even though it has that effect too). The most successful limit-setting is grounded in the attitude that by setting this limit, I am providing this child the opportunity to grow and mature. When we see limits from this perspective, we serve as an encourager for the child, internally cheering for the child to develop their coping skills when their behaviors are limited. Our tone remains even because I have stepped away from believing I am there to stop a certain behavior for fear that I am seen as an ineffective disciplinarian. I can now have a firm but empathic tone because I realize the goal of limit-setting is so much bigger than one behavior. My empathy is high because I also know that this is going to be a hard process for a child who has learned only destructive coping skills to meet their needs up to this point. What I want most is to see the child work through the limit-setting process to the other side where needs and feelings are expressed and met in a way that furthers the child's development and relationships. For some children, this takes a while. The teacher's role is to get that process moving, not feeling pressured to stop each and every negative behavior in the moment through a power struggle with the child.

Patience is another key factor in the success of limit-setting. Children will need a little extra time to engage their decision-making cognitive abilities when faced with a limit. When a teacher sets a limit, the limit may need to be restated a few times to focus the child on the decision to follow the limit. Consider the following scenario. Julia, a 6-year-old girl in first grade, is excited about the glue, takes off the top, and starts to pour the glue on and off the paper. She is singing loudly as she pours. Ms. Alvarado sets the limit, "Julia, you are so excited about that glue, but the glue is not for pouring on the table. You can pour it on the paper." Julia appears to not hear Ms. Alvarado. Ms. Alvarado says again, "Julia, you are really excited but the glue is not for pouring on the table. You can pour it on the paper." Julia hears Ms. Alvarado this time and says, "But I want the glue to cover the whole paper." Ms. Alvarado responds, "You have a plan for the glue but the glue is not for the table. You can keep pouring it on the paper." Julia responds, "I'll just pour right up to the end of the paper." In this scenario, Julia's excitement overrides her attention to Ms. Alvarado's limit. As Ms. Alvarado responds calmly, firmly, and consistently, Julia is able to tune in to the limit and engage in decision-making and with Ms. Alvarado. If Ms. Alvarado had raised her voice in the second limit or stood up to stop Julia, Julia would have likely had a startled reaction and be unable to engage in her own decision-making process. Through Ms. Alvarado's calmness and patience, Julia makes a choice that is deliberate and constructive. It is typically advised that teachers set a limit two to three times before moving to more advanced limit-setting. This allows for the child's focus and cognitive processing to move into place for decision-making. Another helpful hint from this scenario is that Ms. Alvarado uses Julia's name to gain her attention. The use of a child's name to start a limit works to gain their attention and personalize the interaction.

Choice-giving: An advanced limit-setting technique. One tool that extends limit-setting while still honoring the goals of facilitating constructive decision-making is choice-giving. If used skillfully and with the attitudes in place, ACT is a successful limit-setting method for most situations. However, there may be times when children do not respond to ACT and teachers will need to enact the advanced limit-setting method of choice-giving. In choice-giving, the teacher seeks to identify choices that will engage the child in decision-making yet still allow for the child's desires and needs to be met. In choice-giving, the teacher states a choice between two actions, both of which are acceptable to the teacher. For example, The PlayBreak time is over and the teacher has set the limit, "You want to keep playing but our time is up in the playroom today, you can play in here next Tuesday." When the child does not follow the limit, the teacher offers the choice, "You really want to keep playing but our time is up. You can choose to put the zebra in the sand or on the shelf." In providing choices, the teacher always selects choices that are acceptable to the teacher, not wishing the child would choose one over the other. Choice-giving sends several positive messages to the child including that the teacher trusts the child to make choices, the teacher cares about how hard it is for the child to follow the limit, and the teacher is there to journey with the child during the process. Choice-giving also facilitates the child's decision-making abilities by modeling that there are always multiple ways to get their needs met and so it is safe to engage in creative problem-solving. As with all other responses, intentional wording is key to successful choice-giving. Choice-giving statements are personalized with "you" rather than "It's this or that" because the teacher is emphasizing the child's agency in the decision-making process. Also, choice-giving statements include the specific words "choose" or "decide" in order to emphasize that the children will need to think about their own decisions and their responsibility in making those decisions. Instead of "you can draw on the paper or the whiteboard" in which it is stated as a decision by the teacher (encouraging external locus of control), the teacher would give a choice by stating, "You can decide to draw on the paper or decide on the whiteboard" (encouraging internal locus of control). Instead of "why don't you paint the paper or the easel?," the teacher can give a choice of "You can choose to paint the paper on the table or choose the paper on the easel." For students who are struggling with limits, choices help to re-engage them in the decision-making process with the relational support of the teacher.

Barriers to limit-setting. Consistent with the earlier discussions on unconditional positive regard and encouragement, limit-setting assists the child's development of internal locus of control, internal motivation to engage in behaviors that develop maturity and self-enhancement. Common ways that adults deliver limits result in the opposite effect which undermines the limit-setting process. One of the most ineffective limit-setting methods is the use of threats. In addition to being antithetical to relationship-building, threats are practically ineffective as a means of setting limits. First, threats regarding consequences of behaviors are likely to initiate an emotional reaction from a child, thereby another way to take them offline from engaging in decision-making. When a child (or any person) is threatened, the brain engages in deep brain connection (amygdala) and operates from an emotional place (Porges, 2021). When a teacher sets a limit by saying, "If you throw that ball, you will lose recess today." The threat derails the child's cognitive ability to think through their actions and engages in a reaction to the threat. For many children, the reaction will be an impulsive fight response which results in the child engaging in destructive behaviors. However, one argument for the use of threats is that they often work to stop behaviors. My response to this statement is that threats appear to work because they are likely to engage the flight or freeze response of the brain in which the child stops the behavior due to fear. But we would want to ask ourselves, What has the child learned from this interaction? Our goal is for the child to cease a behavior because it is going to hurt them, others, their relationships, or their community. But what they actually learned from complying to the threat is that I will stop doing what I am doing when I am scared or when others tell me to, rather than making good decisions for themselves. Hence, the second practical reason to not use threats is that threats teach children only to rely on external control for decision-making.

Using physical control is another method that undermines the limit-setting process for many of the same reasons that threats are ineffective. In a situation in which a child engages in a problem behavior, emotions can be high on the part of both teacher and child because of the risk of conflict that is likely to arise. Tension sets the tone as the teacher engages. Hence, if a teacher physically moves toward a child or reaches out to grab or touch a child, this physical movement is potentially perceived as threatening. As a teacher starts the limit-setting process with a child, the teacher should be highly aware of physical movement and possible interpretation of that movement by the child. This point is especially true with children who have experienced trauma or adverse events throughout their development. Unfortunately, some teachers will inadvertently move toward a child or reach out to place a firm hand on a child with a lack of awareness regarding how the child perceives the situation. The same brain processes take place that we discussed in regard to threat leading to the child reacting with little consciousness, often resulting in a physical offense or defense toward the teacher or others. Additionally when teachers use physical means to ensure that a child follows limits, the child is learning that they do not have to learn to regulate themselves because there will be an adult who will do this for them. Physical constraints of children teach children strong lessons that they are not to be trusted to regulate themselves and others will need to do this for them. For some children, frequent physical restraint used as a disciplinary strategy negates their ability to engage in creative problem-solving and development of appropriate regulating coping skills.

Thus far, we have covered the structure of the play space, the attitudes of teacher, the non-verbal skills, and the verbal skills necessary for the effective and relational PlayBreaks. At this point, it may seem a little overwhelming to put it all together. Preparing the space, becoming aware of our non-verbal ways-of-being, and practicing the skills are critical to preparation for an effectively relational PlayBreak. The next step is putting it all together.

Feelings Worksheet

Identifying and reflecting children's feelings helps children to feel understood, cared for, and regulate their emotions.

Common Feelings for Children

Happy	Upset	Fascinated	Scared
Sad	Confident	Hopeless	Helpless
Angry	Determined	Lonely	Guilty
Frustrated	Proud	Confused	Sorry
Excited	Strong	Bored	Exhausted
Free	Brave	Embarrassed	Tired
Grouchy	Caring	Afraid	Unsure
Disappointed	Safe	Nervous	Dissatisfied
Aggravated	Curious	Worried	

In the following scenarios, practice giving a reflection of feeling.

Von says to you, "I'm the best soccer player on the whole team."

Margo shows you her paper. With a big smile on her face, she says, "Look at my picture."

Eric throws his pencil on the floor. He then says, "This is the stupidest math ever."

Amelia cries as she tells you, "Izzie said my clothes are ugly."

Lucas is struggling with a spelling test. He then lays his head on his desk.

Michael tells you he misses his mom who is in jail.

Hope tells you she is going to get a dog and can't wait to name him Fluffy.

Camila yells, "I hate you."

Playful Education: Using Play Therapy Strategies to Elevate Your Classroom (Ray, 2022)

Limit-Setting

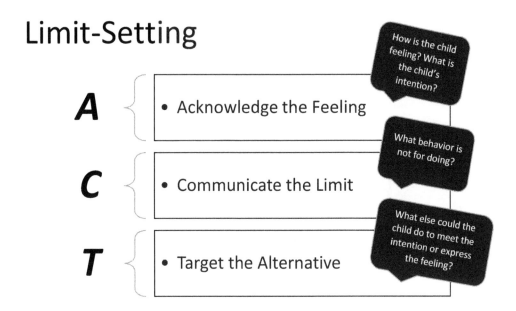

A — • Acknowledge the Feeling

How is the child feeling? What is the child's intention?

C — • Communicate the Limit

What behavior is not for doing?

T — • Target the Alternative

What else could the child do to meet the intention or express the feeling?

Typical Limits to Set During PlayBreaks:

Hurting self	Hurting others	Destroying materials	Destroying play area	Staying in play area	Leaving play area

Examples of Limits:

You are excited about the different color markers, but the wall isn't for drawing on. You can draw on the paper.

You like the way the sand feels through your fingers, but the sand isn't for pouring on the floor. You can pour it over the sandbox.

You want the monkeys to stick together, but the monkeys aren't for gluing. You can tape them together.

You're mad you can't throw the ball at the window, but I'm not for throwing the ball at. You can throw the ball against the shelf.

You want to leave the play area to get your backpack right now but the play area is for staying right now, you can get backpack when we're done.

You're having fun drawing but our time is up in the playroom today, you can draw that picture next Tuesday when we're here.

Adapted from Landreth, 2012, Ray, 2011

10

Putting It All Together: The PlayBreak in Action

Now that we have introduced the selection process, playroom, attitudes, and skills necessary for PlayBreaks, it is time to put it all together to plan for the organization of a PlayBreak. For introduction to the PlayBreak, the teacher will pull the child of focus aside and state a brief introduction on the day of the PlayBreak. "Marquis, today we are going to spend a few minutes playing. Just you and me. We will play right after recess at 1:30." There is no need to do more explaining. Marquis may be curious and ask questions. The teacher can just respond with a reflection, "You're curious about what we'll be doing. We'll get to see at 1:30." At the planned time, the teacher will say to Marquis in a quiet voice, "Marquis it's time for our PlayBreak right now" and lead Marquis to the playroom or play area. When entering the play area, the teacher introduces the room by saying, "In here is the playroom, you can play with the toys in lots of the ways you like." The introduction to the playroom is brief and intentional regarding a balance of permissiveness and limits (Landreth, 2012). By stating, "…play with the toys in lots of the ways you like," the teacher is saying that the child is going to be able to make many decisions but not all actions are permissible. This introduction sets the structure for the presentation of limits at a later time when needed.

Once in the playroom, the teacher sits in one of the chairs while Marquis may begin to talk or play with the toys. The teacher will use the non-verbal skills of facing the child with their full body (remember toes follow nose) and matching the child's tone. The teacher will also attempt to use the various verbal skills. The following is an excerpt from a session.

DOI: 10.4324/9781003285618-13

MARQUIS: *Wow! Are all of these toys yours?*

TEACHER: *You just can't believe all of these toys are here. You're excited.* (Reflection of feeling)

MARQUIS: *This is the coolest place ever. (picks up a shield). What's this called?*

TEACHER: *You're wondering what that is. In here, you can decide what to call it.* (Returning responsibility)

MARQUIS: *It's a laser shield. I can use it to save the people from the bad guys.*

TEACHER: *You figured out how to use it just like you want.* (esteem building/ encouraging)

MARQUIS: *Yep! Look at how I can move it up and down.*

TEACHER: *You want to show me how you can make it work.* (relationship)

MARQUIS: *(as he runs around the room) And I can move it over here or way over here.*

TEACHER: *You're thinking of lots of different ways to move it.* (facilitating creativity)

MARQUIS: *(runs back and forth across the room with the shield)*

TEACHER: *You're running back and forth.* (tracking)

MARQUIS: *Yep! (he throws the shield unintentionally toward the window and hits the window but does not seem to be aware)*

TEACHER: *Marquis, you are loving that shield but the shield isn't for throwing toward the window. You can throw it on the other side.* (limit-setting)

MARQUIS: *Oh, I'm sorry. I didn't mean to hit the window.*

TEACHER: *You really didn't mean for that to happen* (reflection of content)

The session continues on for the allotted time period as the teacher responds with a range of verbal skill responses. When there are 5 minutes left in the playtime, the teacher will provide the student with a 5-minute warning. "Marquis, we have five minutes left in our PlayBreak." The teacher may want to add a 1-minute warning if needed. One-minute warnings are particularly helpful when children are engrossed in their play toward the end of session. At the end of the time, the teacher stands up, moves toward the door, and states, "Our time is up for PlayBreak today." The teacher and Marquis then head back to the classroom.

Special Considerations During PlayBreaks

Although the majority of PlayBreaks will be pleasant play interactions to build relationship between teachers and students, events may not go as smoothly as presented throughout the descriptions provided in this book thus far. Some circumstances require acceptance, patience, and creativity on the part of the teacher. The following issues are common occurrences in PlayBreaks.

Not Playing/Not Talking

For various reasons, some children may not talk or play when they enter the playroom. Some children are anxious and it takes a while for them to feel comfortable. They may be trying to figure out what the teacher's expectations are before they feel at ease to play or talk. Some children play but do not talk during their play. Again, some children may need time to feel relaxed enough to talk. Often, children who play but do not talk are using their time in PlayBreaks to unwind and de-stress. They find the play to be soothing and comforting which can be especially powerful in the middle of a stressful school day. At these times, it is important for teachers to remember that children are expected to speak the verbal language of adults throughout the school day. PlayBreaks allow the child to operate on their own terms and in their own language of play. When children do not talk or play in the playroom, the teacher understands that the child's choice is a decision based on their needs in the moment. The teacher would not be concerned, nor would the teacher coax a child into talking or playing. Using the skills, the teacher would attend to the child non-verbally and recognize the child's intents and actions verbally.

SCENARIO: *Anya, a 7-year old girl in 2nd grade, walks into the playroom.*

TEACHER: *Anya, in here is the playroom. You can play with the toys in lots of the ways you like.*

ANYA: *(stands still looking down at the ground)*

TEACHER: *You're not sure about being here.*

ANYA: *(stands still but glances around quickly)*

TEACHER: *You're seeing what's in here.*

ANYA: *(moves toward the sand)*

TEACHER: *You're moving over there.*

ANYA: *(sits down at the sandbox and puts her hand in the sand)*

TEACHER: *You're seeing how that feels. That feels good to you.*

ANYA: *(pours sand through the sand sifter and watches it as she's pouring)*

TEACHER: *You're seeing how that falls through. You figured out a way to pour it.*

In this scenario, the teacher is limited to verbally responding to what they observe the child doing. However, the teacher is still able to use a variation of responses such as tracking, reflecting feeling by stating, "that feels good to you," or encouraging by stating, "You figured out a way to pour it." During this type of scenario, the teacher slows down in frequency of responding to match the silence of the child. The teacher will still need to respond but at a slower rate than when a child is actively talking. The teacher's tone will also need to be quieter and less animated to match the energy of the child.

Asking Questions

As part of the PlayBreaks, teachers do not ask questions of children because it puts the teacher in the lead with the child following. However, another common scenario is when the student asks the teacher questions. Teachers avoid answering questions during PlayBreaks so that children learn to lead their play and do not rely on the teacher to direct them by providing answers. Some children ask questions simply because they have picked up adult social cues that asking questions is a routine way to be in conversations. They are not necessarily interested in the teacher's answer but they want to be in relationship with the teacher. Other children ask questions to glean the teacher's expectations while other children really just want to get to know the teacher. In the spirit of returning responsibility and fostering autonomy, teachers mostly avoid answering questions during PlayBreaks. Responding to student questions without rejecting the child is a skill necessary for PlayBreaks. Recognizing the intent of the child is helpful in targeting effective responses.

If a child asks, "Are you married?," the teacher would think about the timing and context of the question.

SCENARIO 1: *A 4-year-old child who is playing with two dolls that have been identified as mom and dad suddenly turns to the teacher and asks, "Are you married?"*

SCENARIO 2: *A 4-year-old child is standing by the teacher and picks up the teacher's hand that has a ring, then asks, "Are you married?"*

In Scenario 1, the child appears to be working through something about marriage in her play. She was not thinking specifically about the teacher. She may want to see if it is okay to talk about her mother and father. The teacher may accurately respond by stating, "You're wondering about people who are married." Yet, in Scenario 2, the child appears to be reaching out to build a relationship with the teacher. The teacher may accurately respond by stating, "You're looking at my hand. You're curious about me." In neither case does the teacher answer the child because the child's question has very little to do with wanting to know about the teacher's home life. The avoidance of answering questions does not mean that the teacher can never answer a question. There are times when the student truly wants to get to know the teacher and the teacher is comfortable with sharing information. In these cases, a straightforward answer is the most relational response. In my experience, the majority of questions that children ask are asked for many reasons apart from wanting to know my specific answers. In PlayBreaks, teachers are careful to respond to the intent of the child which leads to more relational interactions and communication of empathy from teacher to child.

Interactive Play

During PlayBreaks, children often want the teacher to actively play with them. Interactive play while allowing the child to lead the play can be a tricky balance. A child may want the teacher to be a puppet in a puppet show, draw a picture next to them, or play a role of a character in a scene. In these cases, the teacher works to keep the child in the lead. There are a couple of tools that work to help with achieving this goal including the whisper technique (Landreth, 2012) and hesitant responding. When a child asks a teacher to play, the whisper technique can be employed which is used by the teacher leaning in and whispering to the child, "Tell me what you want me to say," or "Tell me what you want me to do." By whispering, the teacher is honoring the importance of the play scene by not using a full-volume voice that would likely interrupt the child's flow. The whisper technique is especially effective with young children (4–6 years old) who often do not miss a beat to tell the teacher exactly what to say or do. Older children are likely to prefer for the teacher to use their normal voice to ask the same question so that the child stays in the lead. Once the teacher has used the whisper technique and the child has responded, the teacher will want to engage in hesitant responding. Hesitant responding is when the teacher slows down responses to give the child time to direct the teacher. Instead of jumping in right away which may put the teacher leading the child, the teacher will be slower to say or do as directed if they are unsure of the child's direction. This hesitancy is meant to give the child time to make decisions about the actions they want to happen next rather than relying on the teacher. Whispering and hesitant responding are not meant to frustrate the child but to keep the child in the lead. If the teacher starts to feel that a power struggle is developing in these interactions, the teacher will need to proceed in interactive play with sensitivity to keep the child in the lead as much as possible. The following is one scenario of interactive play with Liam, a 5-year-old Kindergartner.

LIAM: *(picks up the money and food toys). You need food and you have to buy it from me.*

TEACHER: *You want me to buy food from you. You have the food.*

LIAM: *(sets up the food toys behind him and gives money to teacher). Yep! You're really hungry and you need to buy food.*

TEACHER: *So, I **really** need food.*

LIAM: *Yep! Go ahead!*

TEACHER: *Okay so I need to buy food and I have money. (whispers) What should I say?*

LIAM: *You say oh please please please give me food.*

TEACHER: *(responds in same voice as Liam) Oh please please please give me food.*

LIAM: *(in strong authoritarian voice) Nope! You don't have money. You can't have any food.*

TEACHER: *(whispers) What should I say?*

LIAM: *You cry and say you have money*

TEACHER: *(cries as she responds) But I really need food…(teacher hesitates)*

LIAM: *(jumps in) Say you have money*

TEACHER: *…and I have money*

LIAM: *You don't have enough. You'll never have enough. Go away!*

TEACHER: *(whispers) What should I do?*

LIAM: *You cry and run away*

TEACHER: *(cries and runs a few steps from where she was seated). I don't have enough and now I have no food.*

LIAM: *That's right. You only get food when I say you get food.*

In this scenario, the teacher employs the whisper technique and hesitant responding to keep the child in the lead. If the teacher had jumped right into the play without using these skills, it is likely that the teacher may have interrupted the intent of the child. For example, if the teacher had not asked for direction, the teacher may have immediately said with authority that they have the money for food or that the child should give the teacher food because of the money. However, the child's intent was to have the teacher beg for food and to experience the coldness of being rejected while experimenting with the feeling of power. When teachers take the lead in interactive play, they will possibly re-direct the child away from the play that the child is needing to explore.

Going To/Staying In/Leaving PlayBreaks

It is no secret that children have difficulty with transition. Children with behavioral and emotional problems have a particularly difficult time with transitioning from one activity to the next. Even if children enjoy PlayBreaks (which most children do), they will sometimes struggle with the structural transitions of going to PlayBreaks, staying in PlayBreaks, and leaving PlayBreaks. Children may refuse to come to a PlayBreak because they are enjoying the activity in which they are participating in the moment or they need a little extra time to transition. In order to avoid PlayBreak refusal, the teacher will help transition by giving the child a time cue for notice, such as "PlayBreak starts in 15 minutes" or "We're having PlayBreak right after lunch." The teacher may also develop a hand signal or gesture to silently cue the child right before time to leave. While in PlayBreak, the child is expected to stay in the play area with the teacher until the end of the allotted time. Ensuring that the play area has physical structures (e.g., tall shelves, cabinets) to mark the space or is located in a separate room is helpful to signaling the child that the play area is not for leaving. Also, the teacher needs to ensure that the PlayBreak is not interrupted by others. Interruptions send the message to the child that this time is not important and possibly prompt the child to want to end the time. Finally, leaving the room is a very common problem for PlayBreaks. Children enjoy PlayBreaks and enjoy their relational time with the teacher. Leaving the PlayBreak means going back into the classroom where the child experiences stressors and high expectations. Additionally, children sometimes become very involved in the PlayBreak play and have difficulty moving out of their play. The 5-minute and 1-minute warnings are helpful for children who struggle to leave the playroom. Occasionally, the teacher may have to end the Play-Break a few minutes early if the child is taking more than the allotted time to leave the room. In these cases, the teacher does not tell the child that the time is ending early as punishment. The teacher simply ends the time 5 minutes early to have the extra time to go through the limit-setting process without becoming frustrated with time pressures. In all of these situations, the teacher engages in limit-setting and choice-giving to help the child learn to follow the structural limits.

Other Children Wanting to Go to PlayBreaks

A potential common problem in facilitating PlayBreaks with one child is that other students will want to play with the teacher too. Although the teacher may be discreet about PlayBreaks and the play area may be outside of the classroom, other children figure out something exciting might be happening or the child of focus may share their excitement about the playtime with others. Even if a teacher is able to schedule PlayBreaks with more than one child within the same timeframe, it is unlikely that the teacher will be able to have PlayBreaks with every child in their classroom. Some teachers may be able to create a schedule for the school year over which they can manage to see all their children in at least a few PlayBreaks. But most teachers concentrate on just a few students in the classroom who are struggling with problem behaviors or who the teacher believes will benefit the most from the playtimes. Just as some children participate in special services, organization activities, volunteering, or being mentored by volunteers, children who participate in Play-Breaks are involved in an extra activity during the school day. When other children ask if they can have PlayBreaks, a teacher may want to explain how each child is involved in different activities throughout the school day. Additionally, if the teacher implements brief PlayBreak activities for the classroom (see Chapter 12), the teacher can direct inquisitive children to those activities as times for play.

Children with Significant Emotional or Behavioral Problems

PlayBreaks serve to build the relationship between teacher and children on an individual level. Research has shown that special playtimes encountered by teachers and students result in positive behavioral outcomes for children who have exhibited behavioral problems (see Attachment B). PlayBreaks have been used effectively to reduce negative behaviors in the classroom by building positive relationships for students and teaching effective skills for teachers. However, there are times when the child's behavioral and emotional issues are accompanied by needs beyond the relational focus of PlayBreaks. In fact, for a small number of children, PlayBreaks may foster expressive and relational needs that are frightening for the child. Offering an environment of safety and acceptance is ironically threatening for some children who have lived through adverse childhood experiences or trauma events. When children have been violated by adults and have not experienced a trusting relationship, they often have strong negative reactions to an adult who is providing safety, trust, acceptance, and belief in the child as well as providing this type of relationship in a setting where the child is able to express themselves freely. The reaction of some children is to engage in intense aggression, disruptive behaviors, and rejection, all of which may be targeted toward the teacher. Children with trauma backgrounds may begin to play out traumatic scenes or become dysregulated when traumatic memories are explored through play. Children who respond to PlayBreaks with these types of behaviors are candidates for play therapy, a more intense intervention from a mental health professional. A teacher would not be expected to continue in a PlayBreak if the teacher is feeling threatened or in danger. A teacher is not expected to be the child's therapist. PlayBreaks may be hard sometimes due to the need for teachers to engage in limit-setting and the sometimes slow process of children learning to make better decisions. Yet, the ultimate hope for PlayBreaks is that they cultivate joy for teachers and an appreciation of the children with whom they work.

Follow-Up Reflection on PlayBreaks

As a teacher initiates the facilitation of PlayBreaks with children, reflection about the experience is beneficial in deepening the teacher's understanding of the child and growing in PlayBreak skills. Taking time to think about interactions, feelings, and thoughts during a PlayBreak leads to more intentional and effective use of the skills. Although it might be difficult to take the extra few minutes immediately after a PlayBreak, I suggest that the teacher set aside at least 5 minutes some time during the day to actively reflect on the PlayBreak experience with each child. The following are questions that can guide the teacher in pondering more deeply.

1   Overall, what were your general impressions of the PlayBreak time?
2   What were your feelings during the PlayBreak?
3   What were the child's feelings during the PlayBreak?
4   What did you learn about the child during your time together?
5   How did you communicate your acceptance and understanding of the child?
6   What might you do differently during the next PlayBreak?

Reflecting upon the questions alone is helpful but can be even more beneficial if teachers are able to process with one another about their experiences. The support among teachers in facilitating PlayBreaks allows for allies in creative implementation and provides an emotional support for reflection of experiences. When the teacher engages in intentional reflection about their time with the child, empathic understanding of the child and integration of PlayBreak skills come more readily to the teacher. With continued practice of facilitating PlayBreaks and subsequently reflecting on the experience, a teacher will hone their ability to be fully present and have a deeper understanding of the child, while also using their skills with greater effectiveness.

11

The Power of the PlayBreak:
Case Study

In a rural elementary school, Ms. Atkins taught math and science for the fifth grade. Ms. Atkins had been teaching at Meadow Elementary School for 3 years. Meadow Elementary school served an impoverished community and qualified as a Title 1 school with 70% of their students qualifying for free or reduced lunch. Ms. Atkins loved teaching but was having a particularly tough year. Her students seemed to be exhibiting increased behavioral problems and she found herself exhausted as she returned home each night. I started the PlayBreak program at Meadows Elementary and asked for volunteers. PlayBreak was presented as a program that would help teachers recapture the joy of teaching, improve their relationships with students, and increase their classroom skills. Ms. Atkins was doubtful of how helpful the program would be but she decided to give it a try.

In our first meeting comprised of four teachers and myself, I asked each teacher to identify a student with whom they were struggling. This student would become their student of focus and be the student that the teacher held PlayBreaks with for eight times. When I asked Ms. Atkins about identifying a student with whom she was struggling, she hesitated. The other teachers quickly jumped in with enthusiasm. "You should pick Mia." "Yes, pick Mia." "It needs to be Mia." As they all chimed in, there seemed to be some unspoken meaning behind their suggestion. Ms. Atkins responded with an adamant, "Please no! No way!" I could not help but be curious so I asked, "Tell me about Mia." Ms. Atkins responded with "She's awful. She's mean. She's hateful. She acts like a prostitute. Please don't make me choose her." I was shocked with the description. Ms. Atkins had previously shared

DOI: 10.4324/9781003285618-14

her frustration with teaching this year but she had remained hopeful and genuinely caring in her description of her students up to this point. In this description, her whole demeanor changed. She was angry and cruel in her description. It was hard to believe that she was talking about an 11-year-old girl. I responded by saying,

> It's up to you who you choose. I want you to get the most you can out of this program. If choosing Mia is going to be too much for you then I would not advise it. But if you think there's any hope at all for Mia or for your relationship with her, it sounds like she would be a good match for PlayBreaks.

The other teachers chimed in again. "You should definitely pick Mia." "She's the worst." Again, I was shocked with the level of emotion that Mia seemed to provoke in these teachers. Ms. Atkins chose to work with Mia, albeit with the greatest of doubt and hesitancy.

We set up the play time for Ms. Atkins and Mia. We made sure that the play area, which was located in a conference room, included materials that were appropriate for an older child with special attention to creative materials. The plan was for Ms. Atkins to meet with Mia for 20 minutes, use the PlayBreak skills, and have eight sessions over the coming 8 weeks. In the first session, Ms. Atkins brought Mia to the playroom. She introduced this room just as she was taught, "Mia, in here is the playroom, you can play with the toys and materials in lots of the ways you like." Mia stood just inside the door with her arms crossed, staring defiantly at Ms. Atkins.

MIA: *(angrily and accusatory) What is this? What am I supposed to do?*

MS. ATKINS: *In here you can decide. You can play with what's in here in lots of ways.*

MIA: *(same angry tone) This is stupid.*

MS. ATKINS: *You don't like it here.*

MIA: *No, this is really dumb. Why are you just sitting there?*

MS. ATKINS: *You're wondering about how different this place is. You don't like it.*

MIA: *This is just like when we have to line up for math. No one lines up for Math. Everyone wants to go to social studies. Everyone loves social studies. That's a fun class.*

MS. ATKINS: *(her voice quivers a bit) You don't like math but you like social studies.*

MIA: *(raises her voice angrily) No, I said EVERYONE hates math and going to math. It's the dumbest of all of our classes. We don't even learn anything there. It's stupid and we do stupid things. Ms. Rhodes is fun and that's why everyone loves social studies.*

MS. ATKINS: *(no response and sits quietly)*

MIA: *(moves toward the paper and markers and starts to draw)*

Ms. Atkins said nothing else for the remaining 15 minutes of the PlayBreak. Her face looked angry. She closed off by crossing her arms and legs and sat with her back against the chair. At the end of the PlayBreak, Ms. Atkins told Mia that she could return to the classroom. Mia stomped out saying, "Good! This was stupid." I observed the whole play time from just outside the play area. I asked to talk to Ms. Atkins after Mia left. Ms. Atkins was very angry. Before I said or asked anything, Ms. Atkins burst out, "See! See! See how she is. We tried to tell you. Isn't she awful? She's like that every day. Every. Single. Day. How do you even work with a kid like that?" I reflected her frustration.

ME: *You are really frustrated with her.*

MS. ATKINS: *You can see why now. She's like that all the time.*

ME: *Can I ask you a question?*

MS. ATKINS: *Sure*

ME: *When she was talking about math class, was she talking about your class?*

MS. ATKINS: *(still angry) Yes, exactly. She just tries to say the meanest thing she can. So awful!*

ME: *I'm just thinking that if that were me and I taught math and she said those things in the way she said them, that would really hurt my feelings.*

MS. ATKINS: *(her angry face melts and begins to cry) It does. It really does. I try so hard and I've tried so hard with her and she says the most terrible things to me. It hurts and I don't even to know what to say to her. How did she get so mean?*

ME: *I don't know and she seems to really want to hurt you so it makes me think she's been hurt pretty badly herself.*

MS. ATKINS: *(in her thinking mode) Maybe*

ME: *So that was truly awful and I thought you handled things so well considering how hurtful she was. I would completely understand if you don't want to do this again.*

MS. ATKINS: *It was awful but I really do wonder what makes her so mean.*

ME: *(sensing that Ms. Atkins may be opening up a bit to Mia) If you feel up to it, I'm wondering if you would better understand her after a few more play times with her.*

MS. ATKINS: *I'm willing to do it again. I know I gave up during this one so I want a chance to try again.*

ME: *You sound like you really care about how to help her and are doing your best.*

MS. ATKINS: *Well, I try.*

True to her word, Ms. Atkins scheduled another PlayBreak with Mia the following week. Mia was again mean in her comments but this time, Ms. Atkins used her PlayBreak skills throughout the entire PlayBreak. Mia moved to drawing pictures and making craft bracelets. By the third PlayBreak, Mia was softer in her tone. She made a bracelet for Ms. Atkins. She started conversations with Ms. Atkins by talking about her friends and her mom who had died. Ms. Atkins began to experience Mia differently and was softer in her responses to Mia. Ms. Atkins was able to identify Mia's feelings and respond empathically to Mia. In the sixth PlayBreak, Mia came in and sat down at the crafting table. She drew a picture where she identified herself, her mom (who was drawn as an angel), and a very large dark figure with an angry face that she did not identify.

MIA: *This is my mom and she's in heaven. I really miss her but she's watching over me.*

MS. ATKINS: *You're sad about your mom but you feel like she's still protecting you.*

MIA: *She can't always protect me.*

MS. ATKINS: *She's not always there when you need her.*

MIA: *She wants to be but she can't. (Mia begins to cry)*

MS. ATKINS: *(leans toward Mia in a soft voice) Mia, you're really hurting right now.*

MIA: *It's my dad. He makes me do stuff with his friends. If I say I don't want to, he drags me to them.*

It was in this moment that Mia told Ms. Atkins that her father had been making her have sex with his friends for money. This is also when Ms. Atkins learned that Mia's father picked out her clothes so that his friends would like her (hence, the initial cold prostitute description of Mia). Ms. Atkins reported the abuse to social services. Ms. Atkins was the first person that Mia had told about the abuse. Mia was removed from her home but she remained close to Ms. Atkins. It was in the PlayBreaks where Mia was allowed to express herself freely, use symbols of expression (i.e., play), and experience the care and acceptance of Ms. Atkins that her whole life changed. It was in the PlayBreaks that Ms. Atkins learned that this 11-year-old child, who presented herself in rough and cruel ways and who seemed out to get revenge on the whole world, was a child who was being hurt deeply and cruelly by the person who was supposed to be protecting her. It was in the PlayBreaks that Ms. Atkins and Mia formed a relationship that was nurturing and ultimately saved Mia from cruelty beyond words.

MOVING PLAY INTO THE CLASSROOM
AND SCHOOL CULTURE

12

Transferring the PlayBreak Skills into the Classroom

Once teachers have mastered the implementation of PlayBreaks with individual children, the goal is to transfer skills from PlayBreaks into the larger classroom with greater numbers of children. In this chapter, I will focus on demonstrating how teachers can use the skills used in smaller PlayBreaks with their whole classroom and under more stressful conditions. The attitudes that teachers embody in PlayBreaks, including valuing and respecting play as the natural language of children, genuineness, acceptance and prizing of children, striving for empathic understanding, and holding a multicultural orientation are essential to the successful translation of PlayBreak skills from playing with individual children to teaching a classroom full of children.

Student-Teacher Interactions in the Classroom

The PlayBreak has allowed the teacher to develop a deeper understanding and acceptance of a few individual children in the classroom depending on how much the teacher has implemented PlayBreaks. The PlayBreak offers a one-to-one quieter, focused environment that allows the teacher to concentrate on one child. Responding to individual children in the classroom is a different story. It is difficult for teachers to maintain focus on one child when they are responsible for many children. Yet, attitudes and skills from PlayBreaks are transferable to the classroom with a little creativity. First, let's tackle the attitudes. Successful interaction with individual students in

DOI: 10.4324/9781003285618-16

the classroom is dependent upon the same attitudes teachers hold in the PlayBreaks. The teacher values the playful language of children and seeks to be fully genuine, accepting, empathic, and oriented toward multicultural inclusion with every child. Although the teacher is limited in the ability to focus for lengths of times on any one individual child, the teacher seeks interactions that exemplify these attitudes even if they are brief, momentary exchanges. This means that at times, the teacher needs to step back and observe individual children to see what they are needing in the classroom environment. Most teachers are aware of the educational needs of individual students but the question is: Are you aware of the relational needs of each of your students? To start this quest, the teacher may want to develop a weekly schedule in which the teacher spends 1 minute unobtrusively observing each of their students during a free or interactive time. This may seem like a daunting endeavor but in reality it adds up to about 20 minutes a week. During this observation, the teacher will want to notice how the student interacts with others, approaches their school work, seeks to get their needs met, or focuses on their tasks. Jotting down notes about each child during the observation is one way for the teacher to hold the student in their minds and remember the individual needs and characteristics of each student. The observation time is a mindfulness exercise to attune to individual students and nurtures the transition of PlayBreak attitudes into the classroom. As the teacher becomes more attuned to each child, opportunities for meaningful relational interactions are more likely to emerge. The 1-Minute Observation Checklist at the end of this chapter can help with focusing on the types of behaviors and feelings that can be beneficial when conducting observations.

Moving the Skills into the Classroom

The skills that are used in PlayBreaks are especially helpful when the teacher moves them into the classroom. When you become comfortable with using the PlayBreak skills with individual children during playtimes, the goal is to transfer those same skills into the classroom. Although the skills are used in the context of play initially, they are designed to be equally as helpful in building relationships, intrinsically motivating students, and managing problem behaviors in the classroom setting. In order to aid in transitioning the skills, the PlayBreak Skills in the Classroom list at the end of this chapter is a brief reminder of the skills and examples that can be used in the larger classroom environment. One modification you will notice with this skills list is that the teacher will be starting most statements with the name of the student. Unlike in PlayBreaks where the teacher's full attention is on a single child, building relationships with individual children in the context of the classroom involves being specific when you direct your responses to children. Beginning response statements with a child's name lets the child know that you are intentionally building a relationship with them; thereby sending the message that you care about this individual child. Transferring the skills to the classroom can be challenging because of the number of students that you are now trying to attend to simultaneously. However, the use of these skills prevents many behavioral issues that may arise in the classroom which allows for the teacher to be more attentive to individual students.

For example, if Caleb is a student who needs a substantial amount of attention and is disruptive when he does not receive it, the use of tracking throughout the day can potentially prevent Caleb from turning to problem behaviors. Throughout the day, Ms. Rhodes may observe and state, "Caleb, you're checking in your backpack for your snack" and "Caleb, you're going over to Jason's group." These simple statements send the message to Caleb that Ms. Rhodes notices and cares about him. He is less likely to act out for Ms. Rhodes' or others' attention when that need is being met preventatively. The use of encouragement can also be used to build self-esteem and send a message of care (remember to refer to the encouragement phrases in Chapter 9). If Jason becomes disruptive when it is time for math and Ms. Rhodes expects that Jason does not feel competent in math, Ms. Rhodes may use a series of encouraging statements throughout the day, well before it is time for math. Ms. Rhodes may state, "Jason, you really worked hard to get your kick super strong during recess," or "Jason, you kept reading the book even when the words got harder." These statements build Jason's self-concept so that when he enters math time, he is feeling good about himself. For those children who struggle with taking responsibility for their actions, returning responsibility statements set the stage for the teacher to help build positive decision-making. Ms. Rhodes is concerned that Katie blames many of her behaviors on others. Ms. Rhodes starts to begin her statements to Katie with "you decided…" "you're choosing…" or "you chose…" throughout the day in order to emphasize Katie's decision-making skills and raise Katie's awareness of the choices she makes. These types of statements can be sprinkled at any time during the day. "Katie, you're choosing to sit in the red chair." "Katie, you decided it would be a better idea to be second in line." When a teacher starts to use these PlayBreak skills in the classroom, the intended outcome is not instantaneous so patience will be needed. The goal is intrinsic and lasting change. Children will need time to respond to a new way of interacting. It may take Jason a few weeks to begin to believe in himself after hearing consistent encouraging statements. It may take Katie some time to realize she is responsible for both her good and bad choices. As the teacher brings this awareness in a build-up (e.g., Katie, you're choosing…) rather than deficit-based way (e.g., Katie, you have to quit blaming others), Katie will internalize her own agency in making choices and take responsibility for the outcomes.

I would like to share one caution regarding the use of PlayBreak skills in the classroom. PlayBreaks require intentional planning and energy on the part of the teacher. I believe it is tempting to skip the trouble of initiating and implementing PlayBreaks and move to implementing the skills in the classroom. And I believe the implementation of PlayBreak skills in the classroom is potentially helpful even without the PlayBreaks. However, PlayBreaks are where the teacher hones the communication skills with children in their language and in a setting tailored for their needs. In PlayBreaks, teachers will learn the benefits of observation, greater value of play as a language and tool for healing and learning, the significance of the child's relationship with the teacher, and the power of the PlayBreak skills. The teacher will learn how tone affects responses and the child's reaction, how to be creative with responses, and how to deliver limits in a way that children can learn to follow them. These are much harder goals to achieve when the skills are attempted for multiple children across entire days without prior practice. The teacher's involvement in PlayBreaks will provide the practice necessary to know how to effectively transfer the skills to the classroom.

Individual Play Interactions in the Classroom

The combination of valuing play and the relational attitudes of PlayBreaks are integrated through the implementation of individual playful interactions between the teacher and the multiple children in the classroom. PlayBreaks allow for a focused one-on-one time but shorter playful interactions can also serve to send messages of a child's worthiness and significance. The key is to individualize brief play exchanges so that the child feels special in the few seconds that the teacher and child attune to one another. The following is a list of playful activities that are easily implemented in the classroom and demonstrate the value of play and relationship.

1 *Special handshakes.* The teacher may create a special handshake with some children. The handshake is unique for each child and can be created in playful interaction with the child. It's as simple as the teacher saying to the child, "I'd like for us to have a special handshake that we use throughout the day. I'm going to put my hand out to you and you make a way for us to shake hands." During the interaction, the child and teacher will come up with a creative handshake and then practice. Subsequently, this will be the teacher's handshake only for that child. It can be used to greet the child or anytime

throughout the day when the teacher or the child wants to make a connection.

2 *Unique greetings*. The teacher may create a unique greeting for some children that is used to welcome the child to school each day. The greeting can be super simple such as "Welcome, cool dude!" or "Star Wars is the best." The only rule is that it is unique to that student and not shared as a greeting with other students. The greeting should incorporate the student's interest and indicate that the teacher knows the child as a person with individual preferences.

3 *Individual songs*. The teacher may choose a brief song for individual children. The song can include a short lyric or two. It can be a song that is already known or one just created by the teacher. Again, simplicity is best. Singing something like, "Today's going to be a good day" to the tune of The Black-Eyed Peas "I Gotta Feeling" is a way to bring in positivity and fun to a teacher's relationship with a child.

4 *Body bumps*. Body bumps are fun, bigger ways to acknowledge the child and to integrate movement. A body bump could include a hip-to-hip bump, back-to-back, or leg-to-leg bump exchanged between the teacher and child. Of course, these would be light bumps done with playfulness.

5 *Gestures.* Hand gestures can be one of the most helpful physical signals exchanged between teacher and child because they can be done simply and without any other disruption. Gestures can be used when the child makes brief eye contact with the teacher as a way of signaling care without other children even being aware of the interaction. Simple is best. Holding up your pinkie finger to signal "I'm here if you need me," the love sign in sign language to signal that the teacher cares, or shaping the hand in the shape of the first letter of the child's name are all simple types of gestures that are playful and relational.

6 *Jokes.* Jokes are a verbal version of play. For children who are second grade or older, they are especially fun and a great way to play with language. Jokes are an especially relational tool for some children. Setting up a joke exchange between teacher and child wherein each week, the teacher and child will tell a new joke to each other is a way that the teacher is acknowledging the interests and the preferred way of communicating for some children. There are so many joke books so this is an interaction for which there are many resources. Why is 6 afraid of 7? Because 7 ate 9. I love this joke and I learned it from a 7-year-old.

Play in the Classroom

In order to fully reap the benefits of play in schools, classrooms need to be playful environments. An attitude of play starts with the teacher. The teacher sets the tone every day, every month, and every year. Children learn very quickly if their childhood culture and play language are appreciated and embraced by the teacher. In order for playful learning to be implemented in your classroom, ask yourself the following questions:

1 What is my definition of play?
2 Do I believe that play is valuable?
3 Do I play?
4 Do I believe that play is a vital part of my life?
5 Do I play enough?
6 Do I believe play is valuable for children?
7 Do I believe children learn when they play?
8 What do I believe children get out of their play?
9 Have I shown I value play in my classroom? How?
10 What in my classroom demonstrates my value for play?
11 How do children know I value play?
12 Do I play in my classroom?
13 Is my classroom a place where my students have fun while they're learning?
14 Is my classroom a place where I have fun when I'm teaching?

These can be hard questions in the context of our current school environment, especially as children matriculate through the grade levels. Rarely is a fourth grade teacher asked by an administrator or a parent, "How are you implementing play for the students in your classroom?" Yet, research, experience, and life itself show us daily the importance of play for our growth and learning. Under present circumstances, a teacher who believes in the primacy of play advocates, strategizes, and works hard to maintain play in the classroom. Beyond the teacher, playful classroom environments provide time and resources for three fundamental elements: (1) movement; (2) music; and (3) symbols.

Movement

Movement is integral to play for children. Probably the single greatest complaint that children have about school is that they are forced to sit still most of the day. Sitting still is not a natural state for children and sitting still for long periods of time is especially difficult. A classroom set up for movement and activities that encourage movement meet the developmental and play needs of children. Play activities typically involve movement on some level. Some children need room for big movements using their gross motor skills (e.g., running, jumping) while others like to lay down or spread out for play scenes. Even if children are engaged in quieter play such as coloring, they will take breaks to walk around or play something different for a while. Movement is not only a preference for children but we know that movement is healthier for children. When children move, their brains are more active, their muscles are building, their metabolism is increasing, and they are learning body control. The Centers for Disease Control and Prevention reports that over 20% of children 6–11 years old in the United States are in the obese category (https://www.cdc.gov/obesity/data/childhood.html). These statistics were gathered in 2017–2018, prior to the pandemic. Given the growing prevalence of online gaming and learning during the pandemic, recent evidence shows that childhood body mass index nearly doubled following the first year of COVID-19 (Lange et al., 2021).

Movement in the classroom meets physical, developmental, and play needs for children. In a playful classroom, available open space encourages movement and play. Although an empty classroom with completely open space seems to encourage chaos, marked off open spaces within the classroom allow for resting, playing, and moving. Typically, a rectangular space of 6 by 6 feet is large enough to allow reasonable indoor movement. This open space can be part of the play area that teachers set up for PlayBreaks or it can be just a separate space with few materials, soothing colors, and calming music. Children can use the space for big physical movements (e.g., jumping jacks) or planning out and performing plays. Having a designated moving space encourages children to move, interact with each other, and learn to meet their need for movement appropriately indoors. Additionally, setting up the classroom so that larger moving spaces can be made easily allows for special activities designed by the teacher to encourage movement. Can desks/tables be moved out of the way? Can furniture be moved to allow for every class member to stand in a circle? Space in the classroom sends the message that the teacher welcomes movement and play.

Now, that the classroom has the space, it is up to the teacher to integrate playful movement into the day. Many schools embrace a time for movement during their day. At my children's elementary school, the principal initiated a daily break for movement over the loud speaker where students stretched, danced, and vigorously jumped around. If the school does not promote such activities, it is up to the teacher to put in their own movement. A current trend is for teachers to integrate yoga which is beneficial and calming for children. I am an avid supporter of mindfulness techniques in schools. However, I also contend that all children need big, energetic opportunities for physical activity throughout the day. And sometimes recess is not enough. Five to 10-minute physically active breaks every hour are more developmentally appropriate for elementary age children than expecting long periods of stillness.

In addition to opportunities for big, playful motions is the integration of small activities that allow for movement and levity on a smaller scale. Encouraging small-scale play interactions throughout the day help to bring energy and positive feelings to the classroom. One of my favorite resources for these types of activities is the book, *No Props* (Collard, 2005) which is one of several adventure therapy resources that can be implemented in classrooms with very few materials. Adventure therapy materials are often targeted at adolescents and adults but many of the activities can be modified for elementary age children. An example of an easily implemented, quick game with no resources required is the game "1–2–3–4" (Collard, 2005) in which children break into groups of three, facing each other. They each extend their hand in a fist and shake their hands up and down while counting 1, 2, 3, 4 together. On the 4, each child extends any number of fingers up to 5. The goal is that the group reaches exactly 11 (or it could be any number the teacher chooses) fingers spontaneously without talking. Rounds can be repeated as many times as possible and the only rule is that the children cannot say how many fingers they plan to hold out. In an activity like this one, the teacher needs no prior planning and it can be used anytime during the day when the teacher feels a lull or increased stress in the room. In addition to this type of activity providing all the benefits of play, it also offers a social opportunity to allow children to relate and connect with one another. I recommend that a teacher has 10–12 of these types of activities at-the-ready that can be implemented anytime during the day and offers no added stress for the teacher to plan.

Music

Music and play have substantial overlap. Music can be playful and play often involves music. In addition, children love music. Any parent or teacher of a 3- to 4-year old has memorized and sung a child's favorite tune over and over and over again. Alcock (2019) proposed that when we engage with children's musicality, we become more attuned and aware of our relationships with children and can provide more optimal conditions for their learning. Music can be used to promote energy, calm, thoughtfulness, and relational connection. A teacher who strives to implement play and relationship in the classroom can use the dynamic of music to offer a greater emotional bond with children and a sense of playfulness. In the classroom, a teacher can use singing, dancing, instruments, and listening to music to add play to the day.

One way to bring music to the room and build a relational connection with children is to sing children's names. Putting a tune to a child's name when you call them adds a fun tone to the conversation and is a way to help a child feel special. In younger elementary classes, singing names can be a greeting for the day or can be used throughout the day to just notice the child. To expand on this idea, the teacher may lead the whole class in singing each child's name, adding fun notes or lyrics for each one. Singing any song as a class activity is an enjoyable way to make transitions between activities and involve everyone in an activity together. Because students in older elementary grades may be more self-conscious, teachers can ask students to bring in their favorite song that can be played on a speaker for transition times during the day. The sharing of music during ordinary transitions is also a way for children to be exposed to diverse cultural music. The teacher's appreciation of each student's preference for music is a strong message of valuing the student as an individual and builds relational connections.

The availability of instruments in the classroom brings accessibility to both play and music. Drums, xylophones, kazoos, and other percussive instruments (e.g., maracas, tambourines, rhythm sticks) are all instruments that are relatively inexpensive and enjoyed by children. Percussion instruments are particularly suited for both the activity of play and self-regulation. Children will often naturally attempt to regulate through percussive beats. Because the inclusion of instruments can be noisy and disruptive if not planned, the teacher would want to store the instruments in a place out of sight and have a structured plan for when children would be able to have access to them.

A variation of integrating music into the classroom is to encourage dance. Dance combines the playfulness of music and movement in a joyful expression of childhood. During a class break, the teacher can lead the class in creating new dances. A class can create its own dance that bonds the class as a group. For another dance activity, the class can use a break to hold a dance line where children line up on two sides and each student dances down the middle with their own made-up dance. This activity usually results in lots of laughter as children are encouraged to make up wild, creative dances. When conducting these types of musical activities, it is important for the teacher to model the fun aspect, rather than the talent aspect. Children, especially older children or children with disabilities, may be shy to move in front of others. The teacher can model fun by doing uncoordinated fun moves or singing out of tune. The teacher may want to pair children up to dance or sing together or the teacher may want to partner with a child who may be hesitant for fear of being teased.

Symbols and Object Play

Symbols in the classroom are materials that can be used by children for expression. Symbols may be toys or art materials that are readily available to children to express themselves nonverbally. Toys, such as animal families, puppets, and dolls with facial expressions, can help young children express themselves during transitions or free times in the classroom. When symbols are placed in a designated play area, students are likely to gravitate toward these areas when they have free time or need a calming break. If PlayBreaks are held in the classroom, the materials in the PlayBreak area offer a wide choice of symbols. Alternately, if there is not a playroom set up in the classroom, the movement area recommended earlier can serve as a space that includes a few toys to help with symbolic expression. For older elementary students, teachers may want to have an arts station in a designated area where children can use drawing, adhesive, picture, or craft materials to create expressive symbols. Older children also respond to smaller symbols placed around the room or at the teacher's desk such as colorful rocks they can arrange, kinetic sand for creating scenes, or loose legos.

Other objects in the classroom that support the use of play in a mindful and calming way are materials that encourage stress reduction and breathing. Expanding breathing balls, stress balls, pop fidget toys (i.e., pop-its) are quiet movement toys that support a sense of play while also supporting a sense of calm. When teachers set out these materials openly, students are provided with myriad choices for expression to boost self-regulation without the anxiety related to asking the teacher or having other students notice. Allowing children access to materials that provide the ability to express themselves beyond words is a way that the teacher demonstrates an appreciation of play as the child's language.

Integrating play and skills from PlayBreaks into the classroom requires a playful attitude and intentional planning by the teacher. The teacher must first embrace values that support the importance and benefits of play for children. A playful teacher is what makes a playful classroom. A teacher who prioritizes play characteristically moves toward integrating play in the classroom through structuring of space, creating activities, and offering materials that support a play culture. Most importantly, the hope is that teachers are having fun themselves through regarding their own play as a high priority which models the benefits of play to their students. An atmosphere of school systemic support is the foundation to the smoothest integration of play into individual classrooms.

1-Minute Observation Checklist   Date/Time: _____

At time of observation, _____ (child's name) was:

❏ Playing alone   ❏ Reading
❏ Playing with others   ❏ Working on schoolwork
❏ Talking with others   ❏ Other: _____

I noticed _____ (child's name) was

❏ Playing out social play (playing out roles of or with others)
❏ Playing out constructive play (building something)
❏ Playing with objects (what kinds of objects: _____)
❏ Physically moving during their play
❏ Lost in their own play (playing in what seems like their own world)
❏ Sitting quietly on their own
❏ Talking with another child
❏ Other: _____

I noticed _____(child's name) was:

❏ Happy   ❏ Worried
❏ Sad   ❏ Scared
❏ Excited   ❏ Surprised
❏ Angry   ❏ Showing no feeling
❏ Frustrated   ❏ Other: _____

I noticed (write anything else you noticed during the observation):

PlayBreak Skills In the Classroom

Tracking Behavior
- **Use preventatively to notice children individually**
- John, you're moving over to the line
- Sarah, you're picking up that paper

Reflecting Content
- **Use to respond to a child's conversation**
- Jessica, you and your whole family are going to the park today.
- Miguel, you know a lot of things about a lot of dinosaurs.

Reflecting Feeling
- **Use to notice how a child is feeling**
- Robert, you are frustrated with the math problem.
- Jenny, you are so excited about playing soccer at recess.

Returning Responsibility
- **Use to develop a child's autonomy and decision-making**
- Angel, you decided to choose both blue and green because it was hard to pick just one.
- Emma, you want me to decide what's the best picture. You can decide the one you like the best.

Facilitating Creativity
- **Use to encourage a child's creativity**
- Kira, you are finding lots of different ways to use that paper.
- Andre, that can be whatever you want it to be.

Encouragement
- **Use to build a child's self-esteem**
- Amir, you are working really hard during center time.
- Brianna, your crayons kept rolling off but you figured out a way to keep them on the table.

Relational
- **Use when the child is trying to make a connection with you**
- Grayson, you really want me to see your score on the game.
- Victor, you worried that I'm disappointed in your work.

Limit-Setting
- **Use for behavioral issues**
- Dakota, you are excited for recess but now is for standing in line. You can run when we get outside.
- Aiden, you're mad at Jason but Jason isn't for pushing. You can tell Jason you're mad.

13

Integrating Play in School Culture: Building Partnerships with Parents, Teachers, and Administrators

Although determined teachers can find ways to integrate play and offer playful relational experiences for children, the optimal environment for both students and teachers is a playful school. School-wide practices that prioritize play send the systemic message that this is a place for children. A child's way of learning through play is valued and adults in the school are willing to communicate and teach in the child's language. There are many systemic practices that can be implemented to support a culture of play and promote ideal learning experiences. Prompting schools to incorporate play frequently and consistently into their everyday practices represents a cultural shift for many schools. Once again, active and intentional planning positively influences such a cultural shift.

Getting Others on Board for Play

The foundation for building a playful school is gaining support from parents, administrators, teachers, and other crucial staff members. I suggest that one of the first steps toward pulling together this support system is advocating for the value of play. As we have discussed throughout this book, valuing play is not a common part of adult culture. Adults need to be reminded of the benefits, outcomes, and salience of supporting children's play. You may have to launch a play campaign for your school to get people on board. A teacher can start with gathering a few people in the school who already hold

DOI: 10.4324/9781003285618-17

play in high esteem. A play team can consist of a couple of parents, a few teachers, a school counselor, anyone who prioritizes the worth of play in the educational environment. A teacher may want to enlist a local play therapist to be on the team. Play therapists typically love to be involved in projects that promote children's play and may have access to resources that will be helpful in the play campaign. The play team's goal is to create an awareness of the value of play among parents and school staff. Several quick and easy internet resources are available that promote the value of play including the following: https://www.naeyc.org/our-work/families/10-things-every-parent-play; https://www.unicef.org/sites/default/files/2018-12/UNICEF-Lego-Foundation-Learning-through-Play.pdf; http://ipaworld.org/childs-right-to-play/the-childs-right-to-play; https://developingchild.harvard.edu/resources/play-in-early-childhood-the-role-of-play-in-any-setting/. In addition, I have included a handout on the benefits of play at the end of this chapter that can be copied for distribution. In order to gain adult support, adults will need to be able to make easy connections between educational success and play. The play team may want to distribute brief facts or information about play to parents and teachers through emails or internet connection platforms. Beyond awareness, the play team also puts together a strategic plan of introducing and supporting play initiatives in the school.

School-Wide Play Initiatives

Once the play team has been convened and a campaign to raise awareness has been launched, the next step is to develop ideas for play initiatives that promote opportunities for play throughout the school building and throughout the school day. The play team can use their creativity to develop ideas that match well for their students and their communities. In the following pages, I provide some ideas for initiatives that work to inspire a playful school, yet local play team members will be better experts of what initiatives are likely to be successful in their own schools. School-wide initiatives build a play culture in the school so that teachers value the integration of play in their curriculums and instructional delivery, as well as value children's play as a way to grow socially and emotionally.

School-Wide PlayBreaks

A PlayBreak offers a one-to-one experience between student and teacher that concentrates on the individual relationship using the language of play. There is quite a bit of structure in the individual PlayBreak. However, a

PlayBreak can be extended to the entire school. For a school-wide Play-Break, an administrator can call for 10–15 minutes of free play during a school day. Teachers would need to be prepared by having toys and materials readily accessible to the students (see materials suggested in Chapter 7). It is not necessary to have a fully stocked playroom for a school-wide PlayBreak. Offering enough materials so that each student will have the opportunities to explore or play with a few items is sufficient for a school-wide PlayBreak. Rather than emphasizing the individual student-teacher relationship, a school-wide PlayBreak capitalizes on the many benefits of free play for children. The teacher floats through the room as the children play using PlayBreak skills with all the children as the teacher moves from play activity to play activity. Offering the PlayBreak as an official school-wide activity builds a culture supportive of play and provides the chance for teachers to see the many benefits of free play in the classroom. One word of caution for implementation of school-wide PlayBreaks is that teachers would need to be trained in PlayBreak skills in order to feel comfortable with the level of activity that ensues when a classroom of children is encouraged to freely play.

Playful Regulation Activities

Schools have become increasingly aware of the benefits of self-regulation experiences such as mindfulness, relaxation, breathing, and yoga activities. Many schools implement meditation exercises to help children regulate their systems so that focus and learning are enhanced. These activities are typically aimed at addressing the parasympathetic nervous system which serves the person through inhibiting arousal reactions from the autonomic nervous system. Parasympathetic activities decrease breathing and heart rates, lower defenses, promote relaxation, and boost social engagement systems (Porges, 2021). Often, children find meditation activities to be boring. Combining parasympathetic activities with play can be a way to engage children's interests while encouraging healthy development of self-regulation. Teaching parasympathetic play activities to administrators, teachers, parents, and children assist in building a school culture that promotes regulation through play. When children and adults learn these activities, they can typically use them anytime and anywhere to regulate themselves. Children are more likely to use them when they seem fun but I have found that adults also seem to enjoy the playful aspects of using them. Playful parasympathetic activities can be applied in a multitude of scenarios such as when a child becomes angry with another child, a child is anxious about a test, a teacher becomes annoyed with a child's behavior, a teacher is meeting with an angry parent, a parent is frustrated with their child, and on and on.

When these types of activities are used regularly with the whole class, the school moves toward setting up a culture wherein children will naturally use them when in distress individually without feeling self-conscious. Many of these parasympathetic activities, sometimes referred to as self-regulation or self-compassion techniques, can be found on the internet. I provide just a few below.

1   Blowing on a pinwheel
2   Blowing bubbles
3   Drawing – all you need is crayons and paper
4   Rainbow breathing. Hold arms fully extended out to the sides. As you bring your arms up over your head, take a deep inhaling breath. Imagine that you are painting a rainbow as you are going up. As you exhale, slowly lower your arms pretending that you are painting a rainbow on your way down. Do this three times. Having a big picture of a rainbow can be a helpful visual aid for this activity.
5   Shark breathing. Place your hand at your forehead with fingers pointing up like a shark fin. Take a deep breath in. Lower your fin to your heart while taking a slow breath out. Bring fin back up to forehead while taking deep breath in. Repeat 3–5 times. Having a big picture of a shark with a fin can be a helpful visual aid for this activity.
6   Balloon breathing. Pretend you're holding a big balloon in your hands. Extend your hands out as you breathe in and expand the balloon. As you let the air out of your balloon, exhale as you bring your hands together. Make the sound you think the balloon would make as it deflates. Repeat 3–5 times.
7   Face games. Make eye contact with the child. Make a funny face and ask child to copy. Then ask child to make a funny face that you copy. Do this back and forth 3–5 times.

All of these playful activities can be done alone or with another person. When a teacher participates in the activity with the student, they are taking advantage of co-regulation which provides the opportunity for the child to regulate to the teacher's calm presence. The modeling of regulation by the teacher is essential to the success of a child learning and using regulation activities. Kristin Neff (https://self-compassion.org/exercise-4-supportive-touch/) suggests several self-compassion touch techniques that may not be considered play but can be helpful in the regulation process, especially for older children and adults. These techniques use movement and can be used anytime without materials or preparation. I find these to be useful to help teachers, administrators, and counselors with regulation under stressful conditions.

Cooperative Activities

Much of this book has been dedicated to the value of free, self-directed play for children to build relationships and promote optimal development. Alternately, structured and organized play is also a category of play that is part of the overall play spectrum. Developing a school play culture involves embracing all types of play. Cooperative large group activities that incorporate play lead to building relationships and social skills. Considering schools' concerns regarding children's inability to manage interpersonal conflict, initiating cooperative large group activities can be a fun and non-threatening method for building social competence. Mark Collard (2005; 2018; 2021) and Nathan Folan (2012) have published a series of books that provide instructions for activities that can be done indoors and outdoors, with and without materials. These books tend to have a focus on older children to adults but many of the activities can be used with young children or slightly modified to fit the developmental needs of younger children. The activities emphasize movement, interaction, and a playful approach. Collard also operates a creative website that helps schools find cooperative activities that will work for them (https://www.playmeo.com/). These activities can be included as part of classroom activities but they can also become part of the overall school culture by facilitating activities during extra recess time or physical education classes. Schools can implement these activities during a field day or a parent-child activity day. The laughter that ensues when children and adults participate in cooperative play activities is priceless.

Field Days

Field days are one form of play that appears to have survived the changes to academic curriculums. Many schools honor the field day tradition by scheduling a day of competitive and cooperative games. Field days are treasured by children and anticipated with great excitement. I would venture to claim that children look forward to field days for two main reasons: it is play and it is outside. In many schools, field days are scheduled toward the end of the school year and they serve as an ending celebration. The honoring of the field day tradition is an indicator that schools value play, even if it is for only 1 day. The anticipation of field days represents how valued play is for children and the school's implementation of field days serves as relational response to children's needs. The internet is filled with ideas for field days (just google "school field day") that offer creative activities, necessary materials, and proposed schedules for a successful field day. When schools work toward embracing a play culture, one consideration may be increasing the number of field days. Because field days are usually school-wide, field days bring everyone together to value social interaction and play. Increasing the number of field days to 2–3 a year increases the enculturation of the school to value play as a normal part of learning.

Recess

I would be remiss if I wrote a book on the importance of play in schools and did not devote energy and effort into advocating for recess. Recess is the only scheduled time in most schools that supports the free and autonomous play of children. The short amount of time that children are in recess each day is probably one of the most, if not the most, educational experience of their school day. I was recently walking through the schoolyard during recess and stopped to observe three children playing. Two girls and a boy in third grade were in the corner of the yard practicing doing cartwheels. The boy was determined to learn how to do a cartwheel and was pretty bad at it. The girls appeared to be pretty good at it. The two girls would show by example how to do a cartwheel and then the boy would try and he would just kind of flop over. They tried modeling the cartwheels several times to no avail. The boy was becoming frustrated. One of the girls then said, "Let's try this. You try to stand on your hands and we'll hold you up." The boy reluctantly agreed and then moved to stand on his hands. As he moved, one girl grabbed his legs to help pull them up and the other girl grabbed his waist to hold him steady. The three of them went through a very awkward and slow motion cartwheel. The boy emerged from the cartwheel with a huge smile on his face. And he said, "Let's do it again." This time, they went a bit faster and he was more in charge of his body. They repeated the action five times and the boy got it. At the end, the three of them were doing simultaneous cartwheels (admittedly the girls' cartwheels were still much stronger). This whole scene took place in a 15-minute time period. As I have shared in previous play examples, the learning taking place during this play time was immeasurable. Social skills, empathy, value of exercise, value of being outside, building of self-confidence, and learning to manage the physical self were all in play. There was no teacher involvement at all during this interaction. The children could be trusted to instinctually merge learning and play while at recess.

A significant amount of research supports the benefits of frequent and regularly scheduled recess throughout the elementary school years. McNamara

(2019) noted that recess is an essential feature of schools that allows for children to play with peers, create their own games, and make autonomous decisions about their level of activity. Holmes et al. (2006) found that preschoolers exhibited higher levels of attention in class following periods of recess while Brez and Sheets (2017) had similar findings for children in third to fifth grades. Pellegrini and Bohn (2005) highlighted the research matching recess with higher school adjustment, peer relationships, and achievement. Schools that schedule recess time capitalize upon the important factors that recess has been shown to provide including cognitive breaks, physical activity, and social and emotional development. Ways to enhance recess may include providing free play space and guided activities to allow for children to make choices. Also, junior recess leaders made up of older elementary schools students can help to engage younger children in activities and role model appropriate interactions (McNamara, 2019) to capitalize on play between children of various age groups. Barros et al. (2009) found that children, 8–9 years old, who participated in recess at least once a day for over 15 minutes were rated by teachers with significantly less classroom behavioral problems. Interestingly, Barros et al.'s team also found that children who were not provided recess breaks were more likely to be Black, lower income, and living in urban areas, indicating social justice issues related to access to play. The school's commitment to recess reflects its cultural attunement to children across age, identity, and circumstances.

Child-Parent Play Activities

The activities listed in this chapter have focused mostly on activities that are facilitated during the school day with school staff and students. Yet, the inclusion of parents into a play culture is vital to the endurance of valuing play. A successful play team will strategically involve parents in activities, events, and experiences in order for systemic changes to take hold. If field days are increased to more than one a year, one field day could be a student-parent field day in which both children and adults participate in the games. Regulation activities can be video recorded and sent home to parents as a fun activity to do with their child. Cooperative or regulation games can be set up at several stations during an open house. PTA or PTO meetings can start with a simple, quick game. The school counselor can send home a play activity idea per week for parents to do with their child. The school can choreograph a school gesture that students, parents, teachers, and school staff use to greet each other. Integrating play activities into parent interaction with the school encourages parent participation and engages parents in their child's education in a more interactive way. Teachers and administrators are some of the most creative people I know; thus, the possibilities are endless on how to engage parents in playful practices.

On the classroom level, teachers can involve parents in play through materials and playful actions. During open houses, a teacher may leave out materials and instructions for a parent to undertake a math lesson that uses play or facilitate a playful literary activity. For parent-teacher conferences, a teacher may want to set out manipulative toys, such as stress balls and pop-its, a glitter liquid magic wand, or possibly even a small sand tray close to where the parents sit. It is natural for adults to move toward such items when they are readily available. Parents can be encouraged to develop playful good-bye gestures and play rituals for student drop-off and pick-up. A teacher may create a playful dance at drop-off and pick up for parents to see. Threading these activities through multiple avenues where parents interact with schools helps parents develop a value for play and see its benefits for their children.

Teacher Professional Development for Play

Because play is devalued in the adult culture, holding playful attitudes and generating creative play ideas may not be a natural inclination for some teachers. Much of teacher education is focused on developing lesson plans, meeting curriculum standards, and navigating standardized testing. This focus often suppresses creative instincts and narrows the possibilities of how play can be integral to teaching. In order to support a play culture in schools, teachers will need professional development opportunities to expand their thinking about how play fits with what they do every day. Providing resources and support for PlayBreaks is one key to increasing understanding and attitudes favorable to play. When teachers implement individual PlayBreaks with children, they will likely develop a greater awareness of the benefits of play and how play can complement their classroom goals. Therefore, professional development includes providing substitutes or school staff to supervise classrooms when a teacher is in a PlayBreak. Professional development also includes providing time and opportunities for teachers to process their experiences together because learning takes place during those conversations. Additionally, administrators may consider training support for school counselors to facilitate the implementation of PlayBreaks or paying consulting/training fees for play therapists who are trained to implement PlayBreaks.

Another essential training component to building a play culture is supporting teachers in joining play with the curriculum. Administrators support this endeavor by seeking curriculums that use a play-based approach and then providing resources for training in these curriculums. There are many play-based approaches to learning across the academic curriculum that can be integrated to meet standards. Teachers will need access to clear and detailed training on how to use play activities to teach basic curriculum. Once play is fully integrated into classroom lessons, child-teacher interactions, and school practices, the benefits of learning and social-emotional growth are evident.

A final note on supporting teachers toward a play culture is that teachers will need to *feel* playful to send a message of valuing play. The playful attitude is fostered or quelled by school leadership. Administrators who value play model playful attitudes and relational connections. Just as a teacher may implement fun gestures or songs with their students, administrators may want to offer playful greetings, acquiring feedback through games, holding play days during professional development days, or starting staff meeting with a quick play activity or game. I have been in schools for a long time so I know you might be thinking, "Please no! Don't waste my time with frivolous goofing off" or "I can't wait to hear the groans when my principal starts to play a game with us." I concede that these are legitimate responses. But in defense of a playful approach to administration, I will say that I believe teachers respond this way when they do not experience a genuine desire to use play as a connecting point, as a way to build relationships and support one another. Playful activities are often used as one-time activities that are introduced because administrators feel they "should" use them or as a way to placate a small group of teachers or even the school counselor. When play activities are introduced under these conditions, they will likely be met with resistance because teachers sense the inauthenticity and lack of commitment to making a true change to the culture. Under those conditions, the play activity is a true waste of time. However, when administration is committed to seeing the value of play for all members of the school and eager to blend play with the desire to build trusting and safe relationships throughout the school, teachers are likely to get on board, if not immediately, then eventually. If play has not been previously embraced as a priority for learning, teachers will need time to see the benefits and outcomes in order to experience attitudinal changes.

Why Play in School?

When children play, they learn. When children learn, they grow. When children grow, they thrive.

CHILDREN PRACTICE MATH IN PLAY

- How many blocks do I line up on each row and column to build this house?
- Will a circle or square work best to hold this structure up?
- How many seconds faster do I have to run to win this game?

CHILDREN PRACTICE LANGUAGE IN PLAY

- My puppet show needs a beginning, a middle, and an end.
- What words are the best ones to describe my play scene?
- I have a new joke or riddle to tell you.

CHILDREN PRACTICE BRAIN DEVELOPMENT IN PLAY

- I'm pretending to be an astronaut just like Neil Armstrong on the moon.
- I'm going to practice this ball trick until I can do it really well.
- Having fun helps me think better.

CHILDREN PRACTICE CREATIVE THINKING FOR FUTURE PROBLEM-SOLVING

- I can make the sand stick together if I use 2 cups of water.
- I found 5 different ways to save the dolphin from drowning.
- I used pipe cleaners and tape to build a zoo.

CHILDREN PRACTICE BUILDING THEIR SOCIAL SKILLS IN PLAY

- The baby elephant is sad that the baby turtle got hurt.
- There's only 1 magic wand so we have to share.
- My friend made up this rule for the game but I want a different rule.

CHILDREN PRACTICE REGULATING THEMSELVES IN PLAY

- I wanted to cry when the cash register wouldn't open but I found a spoon to open it.
- I'm so mad I want to hit someone, but I can paint instead.
- Pouring the sand through my fingers feels good on my hands.

CHILDREN PRACTICE BUILDING SELF-ESTEEM IN PLAY

- I kept working on the wall until I figured out how to make it stand.
- I'm proud that I kept playing the drum until it sounded just like I wanted.
- I made up a whole new game that was fun.

Dee C. Ray & Amber-Lea Martinez

Bringing Back the Joy:
Concluding Thoughts

Much of this book was dedicated to the ways in which play and relationship benefit children. PlayBreaks are designed to support children to build emotional regulation, social skills, relationships, and learning. Integrating play into classrooms and across the entire school builds safe and developmentally appropriate learning cultures for children. After all, schools exist for the betterment of children. But there is one issue that cannot be ignored. Children can only feel safe and supported in a play environment when their teachers feel safe to promote and design playful relationships.

Teacher attrition has historically been an issue in the U.S. with 8% leaving the profession each year (Carver-Thomas & Darling-Hammond, 2017). In a recent poll by the National Education Association (https://www.nea.org/sites/default/files/2022-02/NEA%20Member%20COVID-19%20Survey%20Summary.pdf), 90% of responding teachers reported that burnout is a very or somewhat serious issue for educators. In fact, burnout was the number one issue of concern for teachers, coming in as a more salient issue than teacher pay. Since the pandemic, teachers are reporting longer work hours (Gicheva, 2022) and higher levels of depression (Steiner & Woo, 2021), especially compared to other U.S. working adults. The number of teachers who plan to leave the profession early doubled from July 2020 to January 2022 (https://www.nea.org/sites/default/files/2022-02/NEA%20Member%20COVID-19%20Survey%20Summary.pdf). Yet, attrition rates have not increased (Barnum, 2022) which means teachers are staying in a profession in which they experience high levels of stress and burnout.

DOI: 10.4324/9781003285618-18

The increased focus on standardized testing and school performance, workload and longer hours, parent demands, and the unforeseen stressors related to the pandemic mean that today's teachers are under more stress than ever. Yet, most teachers persevere through the challenges and show up for their students every day. Their commitment to their children and their profession is admirable; hence, finding ways to make the job more enjoyable is necessary. When most teachers decided to become educators, they were inspired by the idea that facilitating the learning and growth of children would be its own reward. Years down the road, teachers may find this initial inspiration waning in the face of overwhelming obstacles. I believe this is where play comes into the picture.

The PlayBreak and integrating playfulness into the school culture are practices that not only support the learning and relationships of the child but also elevate the relational and light-heartedness of the school as a workplace. People who play together laugh together. People who play together build relational connectivity through both brain and emotional processes. When a teacher plays with a child, the teacher's brain is just as relationally stimulated as the child's brain. When teachers play with one another, they build a support network that is focused on the positive aspects of the profession. When teachers experience playfulness in their interactions with administrators, they feel more relaxed in their job responsibilities, and therefore released to reach their full potential as teachers. And I think we can all agree that teachers and parents could use a little more playfulness in their relationships with each other as they both serve as the primary adults in children's lives, charged with supporting each other for the benefit of the child.

So, in ending this book, I would like to ask, Are you having fun in your job? Do you enjoy going to work each day? Do you have fun when you interact with children? Do you have fun when you interact with your colleagues and administrators? Do you enjoy working with parents? How much play do you find in your job from day-to-day? I am guessing most teachers would answer with a "sometimes" or "with some people." My work and research with teachers has shown that teachers report feeling better about their jobs when they facilitate PlayBreaks. They have better understanding of their students, feel closer to their students, and feel more competent in their teaching skills. Teachers share the smiles and laughs that they experience with their students in play to make their job more gratifying. Given that you have a desire to continue in the teaching profession and that you are committed to the development of students, I hope that engaging in Play-Breaks and playful activities will be a road to bringing more daily joy to your work.

Attachment A

Research on the Effectiveness of Play Therapy in the Schools

Study	Description
Blalock, S. M., Lindo, N., & Ray, D. C. (2019). Individual and group child-centered play therapy: Impact on social-emotional competencies. *Journal of Counseling & Development, 97*(3), 238–249.	*Sample:* 56 children referred for disruptive behaviors; ages 5–10 *Outcome:* Increases in social competence and self-regulation
Blanco, P. J., Holliman, R. P., Carroll, N. C. (2019). The effect of child-centered play therapy on intrinsic motivation and academic achievement of at-risk elementary school students. *Journal of Child and Adolescent Counseling, 5*(3), 205–220. https://doi.org/10.1080/23727810.2019.1671758	*Sample:* 42 children labeled academically at-risk; ages 6–7 *Outcome:* Increases in academic achievement
Blanco, P. J., Holliman, R. P., Ceballos, P. L., & Farnam, J. L. (2019). Exploring the impact of child-centered play therapy on academic achievement of at-risk kindergarten students. *International Journal of Play Therapy, 28*(3), 133–143. https://doi.org/10.1037/pla0000086	*Sample:* 36 children meeting criteria for being at-risk; ages 5–6 *Outcome:* Increases in academic achievement
Blanco, P., Holliman, R., Farnam, J., & Pena, A. (2018) Effect of child-centered play therapy on academic achievement with normal functioning school children. *Journal of Counseling Research and Practice, 3*(1), 1–15.	*Sample:* 50 typically functioning children; ages 7–8 *Outcome:* Increases in academic achievement
Blanco, P. J., Holliman, R. P., Muro, J. H., Toland, S., & Farnam, J. L. (2017). Long term child-centered play therapy effects on academic achievement with normal functioning children. *Journal of Child and Family Studies, 26*(7), 1915–1922. https://doi.org/10.1007/s10826-017-0701-0	*Sample:* 23 typically functioning children; first graders *Outcome:* Increases in academic achievement

(Continued)

Study	Description
Blanco, P. J., Muro, J. H., Holliman, R., Stickley, V. K., & Carter, K. (2015). Effect of child-centered play therapy on performance anxiety and academic achievement. *Journal of Child and Adolescent Counseling, 1*(2), 66–80. http://doi.org/10.1080/23727810.2015.1079117	*Sample:* 59 typically functioning children; ages 6–7 *Outcome:* Increases in academic achievement
Blanco, P., & Ray, D. (2011). Play therapy in the schools: A best practice for improving academic achievement. *Journal of Counseling and Development, 89,* 235–242.	*Sample:* 41 children labeled academically at-risk; first graders *Outcome:* Increases in overall academic achievement
Blanco, P., Ray, D., & Holliman, R. (2012). Long-term child centered play therapy and academic achievement of children: A follow-up study. *International Journal of Play Therapy, 21,* 1–13.	*Sample:* 18 children labeled at-risk by school; ages 5–8 *Outcome:* Increases in overall academic achievement
Bratton, S. C., Ceballos, P. L., Sheely-Moore, A. I., Meany-Walen, K., Pronchenko, Y., & Jones, L. D. (2013). Head Start early mental health intervention: Effects of child-centered play therapy on disruptive behaviors. *International Journal of Play Therapy, 22*(1), 28–42.	*Sample:* 54 at-risk, Head Start students; ages 3–4 *Outcome:* Reductions in disruptive behaviors, attention problems, and aggression
Burgin, E., & Ray, D. (2022). Child-centered play therapy and childhood depression: An effectiveness study in schools. *Journal of Child and Family Studies.* Doi: 10.1007/s10826-021-02198-6	*Sample:* 71 children demonstrating depressive symptoms; ages 5–9 *Outcome:* Decrease in reported depressive symptoms and overall behavioral problems in classroom
Cheng, Y., & Ray, D. (2016). Child centered group play therapy: Impact on social emotional assets of Kindergarten children. *Journal for Specialists in Group Work, 41,* 209–237. Doi: 10.1080/01933922.2016.1197350	*Sample:* 43 children in at-risk category of social-emotional competencies; ages 5–6 *Outcome:* Increases in social competence and empathy according to parent report

Study	Description
Cochran, J. L., & Cochran, N. H. (2017). Effects of child-centered play therapy for students with highly-disruptive behavior in high-poverty schools. *International Journal of Play Therapy, 26*(2), 59–72. https://doi.org/10.1037/pla0000052	*Sample:* 65 elementary children referred for highly disruptive behaviors; ages 5–11 *Outcome:* Reduction in externalizing problems, attention problems, and total behavioral problems reported by teachers. Improvement in learning-related self-efficacy, with no change in internalizing behaviors
Dillman Taylor, D., Purswell, K., Cornett, N., & Bratton, S. C. (2021). Effects of child-centered play therapy (CCPT) on disruptive behavior of at-risk preschool children in Head Start. *International Journal of Play Therapy, 30*(2), 86–97. https://doi-org.libproxy.library.unt.edu/10.1037/pla0000125	*Sample:* 3 children with externalizing behavior problems; ages 3–4 *Outcome:* Reduced externalizing problems for 2 children while 1 child remained in average range
Garza, Y., & Bratton, S. C. (2005). School-based child-centered play therapy with Hispanic children: Outcomes and cultural considerations. *International Journal of Play Therapy, 14*(1), 51–80. https://doi.org/10.1037/h0088896	*Sample:* 29 behaviorally at-risk students *Outcome:* Reductions in externalizing and internalizing problem behaviors
Muro, J., Ray, D., Schottelkorb, A., Smith, M., & Blanco, P. (2006). Quantitative analysis of long-term play therapy. *International Journal of Play Therapy, 15*, 35–58.	*Sample:* 23 children referred for classroom behavioral problems; ages 4–11 *Outcome:* Decreases in total behavioral problems and teacher-child relationship stress
Perryman, K. L., Robinson, S., Bowers, L., & Massengale, B. (2020). Child-centered play therapy and academic achievement: A prevention-based model. *International Journal of Play Therapy, 29*(2), 104–117. https://doi.org/10.1037/pla0000117	*Sample:* 68 children considered academically at-risk; average age 7.6 *Outcome:* Improvement in reading, mathematics, and language usage

(Continued)

Study	Description
Ray, D. (2007). Two counseling interventions to reduce teacher-child relationship stress. *Professional School Counseling, 10,* 428–440.	*Sample:* 93 children referred for classroom behavioral problems; age 4–11 *Outcome:* Reduction of teacher-child relationship stress
Ray, D., Blanco, P., Sullivan, J., & Holliman, R. (2009). An exploratory study of child-centered play therapy with aggressive children. *International Journal of Play Therapy, 18,* 162–175. doi:10.1037/a0014742	*Sample:* 41 children referred for aggressive classroom behaviors; ages 4–11 *Outcome:* Reduction in aggressive behaviors
Ray, D., Burgin, E., Gutierrez, D., Ceballos, P., & Lindo, N. (2021). Child-centered play therapy and adverse childhood experiences: A randomized controlled trial. *Journal of Counseling & Development.*	*Sample:* 112 children with two or more adverse childhood experiences; ages 5–9 *Outcome:* Increase in empathy, social competence, and self-regulation; decrease in behavioral classroom problems.
Ray, D., Henson, R., Schottelkorb, A., Brown, A., & Muro, J. (2008). Effect of short-term and long-term play therapy services on teacher child relationship stress. *Psychology in the Schools, 45,* 994–1009. doi:10.1002/pits.20347	*Sample:* 58 children referred for classroom behavioral problems; Pre-K to fifth grade *Outcome:* Reduction of teacher-child relationship stress
Ray, D., Schottelkorb, A., & Tsai, M. (2007). Play therapy with children exhibiting symptoms of attention deficit hyperactivity disorder. *International Journal of Play Therapy, 16,* 95–111. doi:10.1037/1555–6824.16.2.95	*Sample:* 60 children referred for attention and hyperactivity problems; ages 5–11 *Outcome:* Reduction of child characteristics, emotional liability, and anxiety/withdrawal behaviors contributing to teacher-child stress
Ray, D., Stulmaker, H., Lee, K., & Silverman, W. (2013). Child centered play therapy and impairment: Exploring relationships and constructs. *International Journal of Play Therapy, 22,* 13–27.	*Sample:* 37 children scoring in clinical range of clinical impairment; ages 5–8 *Outcome:* Increases in academic progress and reduction in classroom problems as reported by teachers

Study	Description
Schottelkorb, A. A., Doumas, D. M., & Garcia, R. (2012). Treatment for childhood refugee trauma: A randomized, controlled trial. *International Journal of Play Therapy*, 21(2), 57–73. https://doi-org.libproxy.library.unt.edu/10.1037/a0027430	*Sample:* 31 refugee children with post-traumatic stress; ages 6–13 *Outcome:* Reduction in post-traumatic stress symptoms for children with clinical levels of symptoms
Schottelkorb, A., & Ray, D. (2009). ADHD symptom reduction in elementary students: A single-case effectiveness design. *Professional School Counseling, 13,* 11–22.	*Sample:* 4 children meeting criteria for ADHD; ages 5–10 *Outcome:* Reduction in ADHD symptoms
Schottelkorb, A. A., Swan, K. L., & Ogawa, Y. (2020). Intensive child-centered play therapy for children on the autism spectrum: A pilot study. *Journal of Counseling & Development, 98*(1), 63–73. https://doi-org.libproxy.library.unt.edu/10.1002/jcad.12300	*Sample:* 23 children with diagnosis of Autism Spectrum Disorder; ages 4–10 *Outcome:* Decreases in social impairment symptoms, aggression, inattention, and externalizing problems
Stulmaker, H., & Ray, D. (2015). Child centered play therapy with young children who are anxious: A controlled trial. *Children and Youth Services Review,* 57, 127–133.	*Sample:* 53 children in elevated category on anxiety symptoms; ages 6–8 *Outcome:* Decreases in anxiety symptoms
Swan, K., & Ray, D. (2014). Effects of child-centered play therapy on irritability and hyperactivity behaviors of children with intellectual disabilities. *Journal of Humanistic Counseling, 53,* 120–133.	*Sample:* 2 children with intellectual disability and clinical level of behavioral problems; ages 6–7 *Outcome:* Decreases in hyperactivity and irritability
Taylor, L., & Ray, D. C. (2021). Child-centered play therapy and social–emotional competencies of African American children: A randomized controlled trial. *International Journal of Play Therapy, 30*(2), 74–85.	*Sample:* 37 African-American children with behavioral problems; ages 5–10 *Outcome:* Increases in parent-reported empathy, self-regulation, and social competence, and teacher-reported self-responsibility
Wilson, B., & Ray, D. (2018). Child Centered Play Therapy: Aggression, empathy, and self-regulation. *Journal of Counseling & Development, 96,* 399–409.	*Sample:* 71 children referred for aggressive behaviors; ages 5–10 *Outcome:* Decreases in aggression and increases in empathy and self-regulation according to parent report.

Attachment B

Play-Based Child-Teacher Relationship Intervention Studies

Study	Description
Carlson, S. E. (2013). Effects of a play-based teacher consultation (PBTC) program on interpersonal skills of elementary school teachers in the classroom [ProQuest Information & Learning]. In *Dissertation Abstracts International Section A: Humanities and Social Sciences* (Vol. 73, Issue 8–A(E)).	Intervention: Play-Based Teacher Consultation. 1-day training; play sessions; classroom modeling Single Case Design 8 teachers – K-second grade Outcomes: Decreases in classroom teacher criticism; increase in teacher responsiveness; improved teacher report of teacher-child relationship
Chen, S.-Y., & Lindo, N. A. (2018). The impact of kinder training on young children's on-task behavior: A single-case design. *International Journal of Play Therapy*, 27(2), 78–91. Doi: 10.1037/pla0000066	Intervention: Kinder Training 1-day training; play sessions; supervision sessions Single Case Design 3 teachers – K-first grade Outcomes: Improved student on-task classroom behavior; improved teacher-student relationships
Cooper, J., Brown, T., & Mong-lin Yu. (2020). A pilot study of school-based filial therapy (SBFT) with a group of Australian children attending rural primary schools: The impact on academic engagement, school attendance and behaviour. *International Journal of Play*, 9(3), 283–301. Doi: 10.1080/21554937.2020.1806495	Intervention: School-Based Filial Therapy 3-day training; play sessions Quasi-experimental Group Design 16 teachers/paraprofessionals; 59 children – K-fifth grade Outcomes: Reduced student disruptive behaviors; improved student attendance; increased academic effort and performance

Study	Description
Coggins, K., & Carnes-Holt, K. (2021). The efficacy of child–teacher relationship training as an early childhood mental health intervention in Head Start programs. *International Journal of Play Therapy, 30*(2), 112–124. Doi: 10.1037/pla0000154	Intervention: Child-Teacher Relationship Training 2 day training; play sessions; supervision sessions; teacher coaching Experimental Group Design 7 teachers/paraprofessionals; 29 children – Preschool Outcomes: Decrease in children's total behavioral problems in classroom
Draper, K., White, J., O'Shaughnessy, T. E., Flynt, M., & Jones, N. (2001). Kinder training: Play-based consultation to improve the school adjustment of discouraged kindergarten and first grade students. *International Journal of Play Therapy, 10*(1), 1–29. Doi: 10.1037/h0089441	Intervention: Kinder Training 3-day training; play sessions Single Group Pre-Post Design 14 teachers/paraprofessionals – K-first grade Outcomes: Decrease in student classroom problem behaviors; improved student literacy skills; increased teacher encouraging statements; increased teacher effective limit-setting
Edwards, N. A., Varjas, K. M., White, J. F., & Stokes, S. A. (2009). Teachers' perceptions of Kinder Training: Acceptability, integrity, and effectiveness. *International Journal of Play Therapy, 18*(3), 129–146. Doi: 10.1037/a0015170	Intervention: Kinder Training 2-day training; play sessions; supervision sessions; teacher coaching Qualitative Design 5 teachers – K-second grade Outcomes: Teachers perceived training to be effective and viable for improved classroom management, student behavior, and teacher-child relationships

(Continued)

Study	Description
Elmadani, A., Opiola, K. K., Grybush, A. L., & Alston, D. M. (2022). Exploring the experiences of elementary teachers after completing child teacher relationship training (CTRT): Implications for teaching in diverse school settings. *International Journal of Play Therapy, 31*(2), 71–81. Doi: 10.1037/pla0000163	Intervention: Child-Teacher Relationship Training 12 training sessions; play sessions; supervision sessions; teacher coaching/modeling Qualitative Design 10 teachers/paraprofessionals – Elementary Outcomes: Teachers reported increased cultural awareness, positive impact of training, improved teacher-student relationships and interactions
Gonzales-Ball, T. L., & Bratton, S. C. (2019). Child–teacher relationship training as a Head Start early mental health intervention for children exhibiting disruptive behavior. *International Journal of Play Therapy, 28*(1), 44–56. Doi: 10.1037/pla0000081	Intervention: Child-Teacher Relationship Training 2-day training; play sessions; supervision; teacher coaching/ modeling Experimental Group Design 23 teachers/paraprofessionals, 20 students – Preschool Outcomes: Decrease in externalizing and total classroom behavior problems
Helker, W. P., & Ray, D. C. (2009). Impact of child teacher relationship training on teachers' and aides' use of relationship-building skills and the effects on student classroom behavior. *International Journal of Play Therapy, 18*(2), 70–83. Doi: 10.1037/a0014456	Intervention: Child Teacher Relationship Training 2 ½ days training; play sessions; supervision sessions; teacher coaching/modeling Quasi-Experimental Group Design 24 teachers/paraprofessionals, 32 students – Preschool Outcomes: Decrease in student classroom problem behaviors; increased skills of teachers correlated with decrease in student problem behaviors

Study	Description
Hess, B. A., Post, P., & Flowers, C. (2005). A Follow-Up Study of Kinder Training for Preschool Teachers of Children Deemed At-Risk. *International Journal of Play Therapy, 14*(1), 103–115. Doi: 10.1037/h0088898	Intervention: Child-Centered Kinder Training 23 training sessions; play sessions; supervision sessions Quasi-Experimental Group Design 16 teachers/paraprofessionals – Preschool Outcomes: Increased teacher empathy with individual children; increased teacher skills with individual children
Leung, C. (2015). Enhancing social competence and the child–teacher relationship using a child-centred play training model in Hong Kong preschools. *International Journal of Early Childhood, 47*(1), 135–152. Doi: 10.1007/s13158-014-0117-6	Intervention: Child-Centered Play Training 10 training sessions; play sessions Quasi-Experimental Group Design 60 teachers, 60 students – 3–6 years old Outcomes: Increased teacher communication of acceptance; decreased internalizing child problem behaviors; decreased externalizing child problem behaviors
Lindo, N. A., Taylor, D. D., Meany-Walen, K. K., Purswell, K., Jayne, K., Gonzales, T., & Jones, L. (2014). Teachers as therapeutic agents: Perceptions of a school-based mental health initiative. *British Journal of Guidance & Counselling, 42*(3), 284–296. Doi: 10.1080/03069885.2014.896452	Intervention: Teacher-Child Relationship Building 2-day training; play sessions; supervision sessions; teacher modeling Qualitative Design 18 teachers – Preschool Outcomes: Increased understanding of individual children; improved child behaviors; improved teacher-child relationships; value of training

(Continued)

Study	Description
Morrison Bennett, M. O., & Bratton, S. C. (2011). The effects of child teacher relationship training on the children of focus: A pilot study. *International Journal of Play Therapy*, 20(4), 193–207. Doi: 10.1037/a0025833	Intervention: Child Teacher Relationship Training 2 ½ days training; play sessions; supervision sessions; teacher coaching/modeling Quasi-Experimental Group Design 24 teachers/paraprofessionals, 22 students – Preschool Outcomes: Decreased child externalizing behavior problems in classroom
Morrison, M. O., & Bratton, S.C. (2010). Preliminary investigation of an early mental health intervention for Head Start program: Effects of child teacher relationship training on children's behavior problems. *Psychology in the Schools*, 47(10), 1003–1017. Doi: 10.1002/pits.20520	Intervention: Child Teacher Relationship Training 2 ½ days training; play sessions; supervision sessions; teacher coaching/modeling Quasi-Experimental Group Design 24 teacher/paraprofessionals, 52 students – Preschool Outcomes: Decreased externalizing and total child behavior problems in classroom
Post, P. B., Grybush, A. L., Elmadani, A., & Lockhart, C. E. (2020). Fostering resilience in classrooms through child–teacher relationship training. *International Journal of Play Therapy*, 29(1), 9–19. Doi: 10.1037/pla0000107	Intervention: Child-Teacher Relationship Training 10 training sessions; play sessions; supervision sessions; teacher coaching/modeling Qualitative Design 4 teachers – Kindergarten Outcomes: Teachers reported appreciating skills and training, building relationship with students, and greater satisfaction and competence in their jobs.

Study	Description
Post, P. B., Grybush, A. L., Flowers, C., & Elmadani, A. (2020). Impact of child–teacher relationship training on teacher attitudes and classroom behaviors. *International Journal of Play Therapy, 29*(3), 119–130. Doi: 10.1037/pla0000118	Intervention: Child-Teacher Relationship Training 10 training sessions; play sessions; teacher coaching/modeling Quasi-Experimental Design 46 teachers – Elementary Outcomes: Teachers acquired attitudes, knowledge, and skills consistent with child-centered play; Improved teacher skills in classroom
Post, P. B., Grybush, A. L., García, M. A., & Flowers, C. (2022). Child–teacher relationship training exclusively in the classroom: Impact on teacher attitudes and behaviors. *International Journal of Play Therapy, 31*(2), 97–106. Doi: 10.1037/pla0000173	Intervention: Child-Teacher Relationship Training 10 training sessions; teacher coaching/modeling Quasi-Experimental Design 62 teachers – Elementary Outcomes: Teachers reported appreciating skills and training, building relationship with students, and greater satisfaction and competence in their jobs.
Post, P., McAllister, M., Sheely, A., Hess, B., & Flowers, C. (2004). Child-Centered Kinder Training for Teachers of Pre-School Children Deemed At-Risk. *International Journal of Play Therapy, 13*(2), 53–74. Doi: 10.1037/h0088890	Intervention: Child-Centered Kinder Training 23 training sessions; play sessions; supervision sessions Quasi-Experimental Group Design 9 teachers/paraprofessionals – Preschool Outcomes: Decrease in child internalizing problems, overall problems; increase in child's adaptive skills; improved teacher empathic responding; improved skills in classroom

(Continued)

Study	Description
Sepulveda, C., Garza, Y., & Morrison, M. O. (2011). Child teacher relationship training: A phenomenological study. *International Journal of Play Therapy, 20*(1), 12–25. Doi: 10.1037/a0021938	Intervention: Child-Teacher Relationship Training 10 training sessions; play sessions; supervision sessions Qualitative Design 10 teachers – Preschool Outcomes: Teachers perceived training to improve child-teacher relationships, decrease individual child problems behaviors, increased confidence in classroom management
Schrader, K. L. (2012). The effects of kinder training on students with emotional disturbance and their special education teachers (Order No. 3550084). Available from ProQuest Dissertations & Theses Global. (1284867757). https:// www. proquest.com/dissertations-theses/ effects-kinder-training-on-students-with/ docview/1284867757/se-2?accountid=7113	Intervention: Kinder Training 1 session training; play sessions Single Case Design 3 teachers; 3 students – first-third grade Outcomes: Decreases in negative teacher-initiated interactions
Smith, D., & Landreth, G. (2004). Filial therapy with teachers of deaf and hard of hearing preschool children. *International Journal of Play Therapy, 13*, 13–33. Doi: 10.1037/h0088883	Intervention: Filial Therapy with Teachers 5 training sessions; play sessions Quasi-Experimental Group Design 24 teachers/paraprofessionals, 24 students – Pre-K-Kindergarten Outcomes: Improved empathy levels of teachers; decrease in student behavioral problems

References

Acar, I. H., Torquati, J. C., Garcia, A., & Ren, L. (2018). Examining the roles of parent–child and teacher–child relationships on behavior regulation of children at risk. *Merrill-Palmer Quarterly, 64*(2), 248–274. Doi: 10.13110/merrpalmquar1982.64.2.0248

Alcock, S. (2019). Young children's musicality: Relating with rhythm. In M. Charles & J. Bellinson (Eds.), *The importance of play in early childhood education: Psychoanalytic, attachment, and developmental perspectives* (pp. 118–132). Routledge.

Ansari, A., Hofkens, T. L., & Pianta, R. C. (2020). Teacher-student relationships across the first seven years of education and adolescent outcomes. *Journal of Applied Developmental Psychology, 71.* Doi: 10.1016/j.appdev.2020.101200

Axline, V. (1947). *Play therapy.* Ballantine.

Axline, V. (1964). *Dibs: In search of self.* Ballantine.

Badenoch, B. (2008). *Being a brain-wise therapist: A practical guide to interpersonal neurobiology.* Norton.

Badenoch, B. (2018). *The heart of trauma: Healing the embodied brain in the context of relationships.* Norton.

Barnum, M. (March 9, 2022). Uptick but no exodus: Despite stress, most teachers stay put. *Chalkbeat.* https://www.chalkbeat.org/2022/3/9/22967759/teacher-turnover-retention-pandemic-data

Barros, R. M., Silver, E. J., & Stein, R. E. K. (2009). School recess and group classroom behavior. *Pediatrics, 123*(2), 431–436. Doi: 10.1542/peds.2007-2825

Bennett, M. M., & Helker, W. P. (2020). Adapting CPRT for teachers. In G. L. Landreth & S. C. Bratton (Eds.), *Child-parent relationship therapy (CPRT): An evidence-based 10-session filial therapy model* (2nd ed., pp. 413–430). Routledge.

Bergen, D. (2015). Play, technology toy affordances, brain development: Needs and policy issues. In D. Fromberg & D. Bergen (Eds.), *Play from birth to twelve: Contexts, perspectives, and meaning* (3rd ed., pp. 435–441). Routledge.

Bergen, D., & Fromberg, D. (2015). Play and socialization in middle childhood. In D. Fromberg & D. Bergen (Eds.), *Play from birth to twelve: Contexts, perspectives, and meaning* (3rd ed., pp. 31–34). Routledge.

Bodrova, E., & Leong, D. (2011). Revisiting Vygotskian perspectives on play and pedagogy. In S. Rogers (Ed.), *Rethinking play and pedagogy in early childhood education: Concepts, contexts, and cultures* (pp. 60–72). Routledge.

Blodgett, C., & Lanigan, J. D. (2018). The association between adverse childhood experience (ACE) and school success in elementary school children. *School Psychology Quarterly, 33*(1), 137–146. Doi: 10.1037/spq0000256

Bratton, S. C., Ceballos, P. L., Sheely-Moore, A. I., Meany-Walen, K., Pronchenko, Y., & Jones, L. D. (2013). Head Start early mental health intervention: Effects of child-centered play therapy on disruptive behaviors. *International Journal of Play Therapy, 22*(1), 28–42.

Bratton, S., & Landreth, G. (2020). *Child-parent relationship therapy (CPRT) treatment manual: An evidence-based 10-session filial therapy model* (2nd ed.). Routledge.

Bratton, S., Ray, D., Rhine, T., & Jones, L. (2005). The efficacy of play therapy with children: A meta-analytic review of treatment outcomes. *Professional Psychology: Research and Practice, 36*, 376–390. Doi: 10.1037/0735-7028.36.4.376

Brez, C., & Sheets, V. (2017). Classroom benefits of recess. *Learning Environments Research, 20*(3), 433–445. Doi: 10.1007/s10984-017-9237-x

Carlson, S. E. (2013). Effects of a play-based teacher consultation (PBTC) program on interpersonal skills of elementary school teachers in the classroom [ProQuest Information & Learning]. In Dissertation Abstracts International Section A: Humanities and Social Sciences (Vol. 73, Issue 8–A(E)).

Carver-Thomas, D., & Darling-Hammond, L. (2017). *Teacher turnover: Why it matters and what we can do about it*. Palo Alto, CA: Learning Policy Institute.

Chen, S.-Y., & Lindo, N. A. (2018). The impact of kinder training on young children's on-task behavior: A single-case design. *International Journal of Play Therapy, 27*(2), 78–91. Doi: 10.1037/pla0000066

Christie, J., & Roskos, K. (2015). Play as a medium for literacy development. In D. Fromberg & D. Bergen (Eds.), *Play from birth to twelve: Contexts, perspectives, and meanings* (3rd ed., pp. 191–196). Routledge.

Coggins, K., & Carnes-Holt, K. (2021). The efficacy of child–teacher relationship training as an early childhood mental health intervention in Head Start programs. *International Journal of Play Therapy, 30*(2), 112–124. Doi: 10.1037/pla0000154

Collard, M. (2005). *No props: Great games with no equipment*. Project Adventure.

Collard, M. (2018). *No props No problem: 150+ outrageously fun group games & activities using no equipment*. Author.

Collard, M. (2021). *Count me in: Large group games that work*. Project Adventure.

Collins, B. A., O'Connor, E. E., Supplee, L., & Shaw, D. S. (2017). Behavior problems in elementary school among low-income boys: The role of teacher–child relationships. *The Journal of Educational Research, 110*(1), 72–84. Doi: 10.1080/00220671.2015.1039113

Cooper, J., Brown, T., & Mong-lin Yu. (2020). A pilot study of school-based filial therapy (SBFT) with a group of Australian children attending rural primary schools: The impact on academic engagement, school attendance and behaviour. *International Journal of Play, 9*(3), 283–301. Doi: 10.1080/21594937.2020.1806495

Davis, D. E., DeBlaere, C., Owen, J., Hook, J. N., Rivera, D. P., Choe, E., Van Tongeren, D. R., Worthington, E. L., Jr., & Placeres, V. (2018). The multicultural orientation framework: A narrative review. *Psychotherapy, 55*(1), 89–100. Doi: 10.1037/pst0000160.supp (Supplemental)

Dillman Taylor, D., Purswell, K., Cornett, N., & Bratton, S. C. (2021). Effects of child-centered play therapy (CCPT) on disruptive behavior of at-risk preschool children in Head Start. *International Journal of Play Therapy, 30*(2), 86–97. Doi: 10.1037/pla0000125

Draper, K., White, J., O'Shaughnessy, T. E., Flynt, M., & Jones, N. (2001). Kinder training: Play-based consultation to improve the school adjustment of discouraged kindergarten and first grade students. *International Journal of Play Therapy, 10*(1), 1–29. Doi: 10.1037/h0089441

Edwards, N. A., Varjas, K. M., White, J. F., & Stokes, S. A. (2009). Teachers' perceptions of kinder training: Acceptability, integrity, and effectiveness. *International Journal of Play Therapy, 18*(3), 129–146. Doi: 10.1037/a0015170

Elkind, D. (2007). *The power of play: Learning what comes naturally.* Da Capo.

Elmadani, A., Opiola, K. K., Grybush, A. L., & Alston, D. M. (2022). Exploring the experiences of elementary teachers after completing child teacher relationship training (CTRT): Implications for teaching in diverse school settings. *International Journal of Play Therapy, 31*(2), 71–81. Doi: 10.1037/pla0000163

Folan, N. (2012). *Hundredth monkey activities that inspire playful learning.* Project Adventure.

Freud, A. (1946). *The psycho-analytical treatment of children.* International Universities Press.

Gesell Institute of Child Development. (2011). *Gesell developmental observation: Revised examiner's manual.* Gesell Institute.

Gicheva, D. (2022). Teachers' working hours during the COVID-19 pandemic. *Educational Researcher, 51*, 85–87. Doi: 10.3102/0013189X211056897

Gonzales-Ball, T. L., & Bratton, S. C. (2019). Child–teacher relationship training as a head start early mental health intervention for children exhibiting disruptive behavior. *International Journal of Play Therapy, 28*(1), 44–56. Doi: 10.1037/pla0000081

Gray, P. (2013). *Free to learn: Why unleashing the instinct to play will make our children happier, more self-reliant, and better students for life.* Basic Books.

Gray, P. (2019). Evolutionary functions of play: Practice, resilience, innovation, and cooperation. In P. Smith & J. Roopnarine (Eds.), *The Cambridge handbook of play: Developmental and disciplinary perspectives* (pp. 84–102). Cambridge University Press.

Guerney, B., Jr. (1964). Filial therapy: Description and rationale. *Journal of Consulting Psychology, 28*(4), 304–310. Doi: 10.1037/h0041340

Guerney, B. G., Jr., & Flumen, A. B. (1970). Teachers as psychotherapeutic agents for withdrawn children. *Journal of School Psychology, 8*(2), 107–113. Doi: 10.1016/0022-4405(70)90029-4

Guerney, L. (2000). Filial therapy into the 21st century. *International Journal of Play Therapy, 9*(2), 1–17. Doi: 10.1037/h0089433

Gülay Ogelman, H. (2021). Examining peer relationships of young children in terms of teacher–child relationship. *Early Child Development & Care, 191*(16), 2508–2515. Doi: 10.1080/03004430.2020.1718671

Haight, W., & Miller, P. (1993). *Pretending at home: Early development in a sociocultural context*. State University of New York Press.

Hamre, B., & Pianta, R. (2001). Early teacher-child relationships and the trajectory of children's school outcomes through eighth grade. *Child Development, 72*, 625–638.

Hatfield, B. E., & Williford, A. P. (2017). Cortisol patterns for young children displaying disruptive behavior: Links to a teacher-child, relationship-focused intervention. *Prevention Science, 18*(1), 40–49. Doi: 10.1007/s11121-016-0693-9

Hays-Grudo, J., & Morris, A. (2020). *Adverse and protective childhood experiences: A developmental perspective*. American Psychological Association.

Helker, W. P., & Ray, D. C. (2009). Impact of child teacher relationship training on teachers' and aides' use of relationship-building skills and the effects on student classroom behavior. *International Journal of Play Therapy, 18*(2), 70–83. Doi: 10.1037/a0014456

Hess, B. A., Post, P., & Flowers, C. (2005). A follow-up study of kinder training for preschool teachers of children deemed at-risk. *International Journal of Play Therapy, 14*(1), 103–115. Doi: 10.1037/h0088898

Hirsh-Pasek, K., & Golinkoff, R. (2003). *Einstein never used flash cards: How our children really learn-and why they need to play more and memorize less*. Rodale.

Holmes, R. M., Pellegrini, A. D., & Schmidt, S. L. (2006). The effects of different recess timing regimens on preschoolers' classroom attention. *Early Child Development and Care, 176*(7), 735–743. Doi: 10.1080/03004430500207179

Hughes, J., Cavell, T., & Jackson, T. (1999). Influence of the teacher-student relationship on childhood conduct problems: A prospective study. *Journal of Clinical Child Psychology, 28*, 173–184.

Jent, J., Niec, L., & Baker, S. (2011). Play and interpersonal processes. In S. Russ & L. Niec (Eds.), *Play in clinical practice: Evidence-based approaches* (pp. 23–47). Guilford.

Jeon, L., & Ardeleanu, K. (2020). Work climate in early care and education and teachers' stress: Indirect associations through emotion regulation. *Early Education and Development, 31*(7), 1031–1051. Doi: 10.1080/10409289.2020.1776809

Jimenez, M. E., Wade, Jr., R., Lin, Y., Morrow, L. M., & Reichman, N. E. (2016). Adverse experiences in early childhood and kindergarten outcomes. *Pediatrics, 137*(2), 1–9.

Johnson, J. (2015). Play development from ages four to eight years. In D. Fromberg & D. Bergen (Eds.), *Play from birth to twelve: Contexts, perspectives, and meaning* (3rd ed., pp. 21–29). Routledge.

Klein, M. (1975/1932). *The psycho-analysis of children.* Delacorte.

Kottman, T., & Meany-Walen, K. (2016). *Partners in play: An Adlerian approach to play therapy* (3rd ed.). American Counseling Association.

Ladd, G., & Burgess, K. (2001). Do relational risks and protective factors moderate the linkages between childhood aggression and early psychological and school adjustment? *Child Development, 72,* 1579–1601.

Landreth, G. (2002). *Play therapy: The art of the relationship* (2nd ed.). Routledge.

Landreth, G. (2012). *Play therapy: The art of the relationship* (3rd ed.). Routledge.

Landreth, G., & Bratton, S. (2019). *Child-parent relationship therapy: An evidence-based 10-session filial therapy model* (2nd ed.). Routledge.

Lange, S., Kompaniyets, L., Freedman, D., et al. (2021). Longitudinal trends in body mass index before and during the COVID-19 pandemic among persons aged 2–19 Years — United States, 2018–2020. *MMWR Morb Mortal Wkly Rep 2021, 70,* 1278–1283. Doi: http://dx.doi.org/10.15585/mmwr.mm7037a3

Leung, C. (2015). Enhancing social competence and the child–teacher relationship using a child-centred play training model in Hong Kong preschools. *International Journal of Early Childhood, 47*(1), 135–152. Doi: 10.1007/s13158-014-0117-6

Lin, Y., & Bratton, S. C. (2015). A meta-analytic review of child-centered play therapy approaches. *Journal of Counseling & Development, 93*(1), 45–58. Doi: 10.1002/j.1556-6676.2015.00180.x

Lindo, N. A., Taylor, D. D., Meany-Walen, K. K., Purswell, K., Jayne, K., Gonzales, T., & Jones, L. (2014). Teachers as therapeutic agents: Perceptions of a school-based mental health initiative. *British Journal of Guidance & Counselling, 42*(3), 284–296. Doi: 10.1080/03069885.2014.896452

McMahon, S. D., Anderman, E. M., Astor, R. A., Espelage, D. L., Martinez, A., Reddy, L. A., & Worrell, F. C. (2022). Violence against educators and school personnel: Crisis during COVID. *Technical report.* American Psychological Association.

McNamara, L. (2019). Recess: Supporting a culture of meaningful play at school. In P. Smith & J. Roopnarine (Eds.), *The Cambridge handbook of play: Developmental and disciplinary perspectives* (pp. 686–703). Cambridge University Press.

Morrison Bennett, M. O., & Bratton, S. C. (2011). The effects of child teacher relationship training on the children of focus: A pilot study. *International Journal of Play Therapy, 20*(4), 193–207. Doi: 10.1037/a0025833

National Education Agency. (2022). Poll results: Stress and burnout pose threat of educator shortages. https://www.nea.org/sites/default/files/2022-02/NEA%20Member%20COVID-19%20Survey%20Summary.pdf

Nelsen, J., Lott, L., & Glenn, H. (2013). *Positive discipline in the classroom: Developing mutual respect, cooperation, and responsibility in your classroom* (4th ed.). Three Rivers Press.

Nicolopoulou, A. (2019). Pretend and social pretend play. In P. Smith & J. Roopnarine (Eds.), *The Cambridge handbook of play: Developmental and disciplinary perspectives* (pp. 183–199). Cambridge University Press.

O'Connor, E. (2010). Teacher–child relationships as dynamic systems. *Journal of School Psychology, 48*(3), 187–218. Doi: 10.1016/j.jsp.2010.01.001

Olsen, A. A., & Huang, F. L. (2021). The association between student socioeconomic status and student–teacher relationships on math achievement. *School Psychology, 36*(6), 464–474. Doi: 10.1037/spq0000455

Owen, J. J., Tao, K., Leach, M. M., & Rodolfa, E. (2011). Clients' perceptions of their psychotherapists' multicultural orientation. *Psychotherapy, 48*(3), 274–282. https://doi-org.libproxy.library.unt.edu/10.1037/a0022065

Pakarinen, E., Lerkkanen, M., Viljaranta, J., & Suchodoletz, A. (2021). Investigating bidirectional links between the quality of teacher–child relationships and children's interest and pre-academic skills in literacy and math. *Child Development, 92*(1), 388–407. Doi: 10.1111/cdev.13431

Pellegrini, A. (2019). Object use in childhood. In P. Smith & J. Roopnarine (Eds.), *The Cambridge handbook of play: Developmental and disciplinary perspectives* (pp. 165–182). Cambridge University Press.

Pellegrini, A. D., & Bohn, C. M. (2005). The role of recess in children's cognitive performance and school adjustment. *Educational Researcher, 34*(1), 13–19.

Piaget, J. (1962). *Play, dreams and imitation in childhood.* W.W. Norton & Co.

Pianta, R. (1999). *Enhancing relationships between children and teachers.* American Psychological Association.

Porges, S. (2021). *Polyvagal safety: Attachment, communication, self-regulation.* Norton.

Post, P. B., Grybush, A. L., Elmadani, A., & Lockhart, C. E. (2020a). Fostering resilience in classrooms through child–teacher relationship training. *International Journal of Play Therapy, 29*(1), 9–19. Doi: 10.1037/pla0000107

Post, P. B., Grybush, A. L., Flowers, C., & Elmadani, A. (2020b). Impact of child–teacher relationship training on teacher attitudes and classroom behaviors. *International Journal of Play Therapy, 29*(3), 119–130. Doi: 10.1037/pla0000118

Post, P. B., Grybush, A. L., García, M. A., & Flowers, C. (2022). Child–teacher relationship training exclusively in the classroom: Impact on teacher attitudes and behaviors. *International Journal of Play Therapy, 31*(2), 97–106. Doi: 10.1037/pla0000173

Post, P., McAllister, M., Sheely, A., Hess, B., & Flowers, C. (2004). Child-centered kinder training for teachers of pre-school children deemed at-risk. *International Journal of Play Therapy, 13*(2), 53–74. Doi: 10.1037/h0088890

Ray, D. (2011). *Advanced play therapy: Conditions, knowledge, and skills for child practice*. Routledge.

Ray, D. (Ed.). (2016). *A therapist's guide to child development: The extraordinarily normal years*. Routledge.

Ray, D., Blanco, P., Sullivan, J., & Holliman, R. (2009). An exploratory study of child-centered play therapy with aggressive children. *International Journal of Play Therapy, 18*, 162–175. Doi: 10.1037/a0014742

Ray, D. C., Armstrong, S. A., Balkin, R. S., & Jayne, K. M. (2015). Child-centered play therapy in the schools: Review and meta-analysis. *Psychology in the Schools, 52*(2), 107–123. Doi: 10.1002/pits.21798

Ray, D., Cheng, R., Turner, K., & Aguilar, E. (2022). The multicultural playroom. In D. Ray, Y. Ogawa, & Y. Cheng (Eds.), *Multicultural play therapy: Making the most of cultural opportunities with children* (pp. 279–299). Routledge.

Ray, D., Muro, J., & Schumann, B. (2004). Implementing play therapy in the schools: Lessons learned. *International Journal of Play Therapy, 13*(1), 79–100. Doi: 10.1037/h0088886

Rogers, C. (1942). *Counseling and psychotherapy*. Houghton Mifflin Company.

Rogers, C. (1951). *Client-centered therapy: Its current practice, implications and theory*. Houghton Mifflin.

Rogers, C. (1961). *On becoming a person: A therapist's view of psychotherapy*. Houghton Mifflin.

Rogers, C. (1969). *Freedom to learn*. Merrill.

Rogers, C. R. (1957). The necessary and sufficient conditions of therapeutic personality change. *Journal of Consulting Psychology, 21*(2), 95–103. Doi: 10.1037/h0045357

Roskos, K. (2019). Play and literacy: Knowns and unknowns in a changing world. In P. Smith & J. Roopnarine (Eds.), *The Cambridge handbook of play: Developmental and disciplinary perspectives* (pp. 528–545). Cambridge University Press.

Russ, S., Fiorelli, J., & Spannagel, S. (2011). Cognitive and affective processes in play. In S. Russ & L. Niec (Eds.), *Play in clinical practice: Evidence-based approaches* (pp. 3–22). Guilford.

Russ, S., & Lee, A. (2019). Pretend play in the classroom: Helping children grow. In M. Charles & J. Bellinson (Eds.), *The importance of play in early childhood education: Psychoanalytic, attachment, and developmental perspectives* (pp. 19–32). Routledge.

Sabol, T. J., & Pianta, R. C. (2012). Recent trends in research on teacher–child relationships. *Attachment & Human Development, 14*(3), 213–231. Doi: 10.1080/14616734.2012.672262

Schaefer, C., & Drewes, A. (2014). *The therapeutic powers of play: 20 core agents of change* (2nd ed.). Wiley.

Schottelkorb, A. A., Doumas, D. M., & Garcia, R. (2012). Treatment for childhood refugee trauma: A randomized, controlled trial. *International Journal of Play Therapy, 21*(2), 57–73. Doi: 10.1037/a0027430

Schottelkorb, A. A., Swan, K. L., & Ogawa, Y. (2020). Intensive child-centered play therapy for children on the autism spectrum: A pilot study. *Journal of Counseling & Development, 98*(1), 63–73. Doi: 10.1002/jcad.12300

Sepulveda, C., Garza, Y., & Morrison, M. O. (2011). Child teacher relationship training: A phenomenological study. *International Journal of Play Therapy, 20*(1), 12–25. Doi: 10.1037/a0021938

Shamay-Tsoory, S. (2011). Empathic processing: Its cognitive and affective dimensions and neuroanatomical basis. In J. Decety & W. Ickes (Eds.), *The social neuroscience of empathy* (pp. 215–232). Massachusetts Institute of Technology.

Skalická, V., Stenseng, F., & Wichstrøm, L. (2015). Reciprocal relations between student–teacher conflict, children's social skills and externalizing behavior: A three-wave longitudinal study from preschool to third grade. *International Journal of Behavioral Development, 39*(5), 413–425. Doi: 10.1177/0165025415584187

Smith, D. M., & Landreth, G. L. (2004). Filial therapy with teachers of deaf and hard of hearing preschool children. *International Journal of Play Therapy, 13*(1), 13–33. Doi: 10.1037/h0088883

Smith, P. (2010). *Children and play*. Wiley-Blackwell.

Spencer, A. E., Oblath, R., Dayal, R. et al. (2021). Changes in psychosocial functioning among urban, school-age children during the COVID-19 pandemic. *Child and Adolescent Psychiatry and Mental Health, 15,* 73 (2021). Doi: 10.1186/s13034-021-00419-w

Spilt, J. L., & Hughes, J. N. (2015). African American children at risk of increasingly conflicted teacher–student relationships in elementary school. *School Psychology Review, 44*(3), 306–314. Doi: 10.17105/spr-14-0033.1

Steiner, E. D., & Woo, A. (2021). *Job-related stress threatens the teacher supply: Key findings from the 2021 state of the U.S. teacher survey.* Santa Monica, CA: RAND Corporation. https://www.rand.org/pubs/research_reports/RRA1108-1.html

Stulmaker, H. (2013). Counseling-based teacher interventions: Defining, exploring, and differentiating. *International Journal of Play Therapy, 22*(1), 2–12. Doi: 10.1037/a0030195

Valiente, C., Parker, J. H., Swanson, J., Bradley, R. H., & Groh, B. M. (2019). Early elementary student-teacher relationship trajectories predict girls' math and boys' reading achievement. *Early Childhood Research Quarterly, 49*, 109–121. Doi: 10.1016/j.ecresq.2019.05.001

Veiga, G., Neto, C., & Rieffe, C. (2016). Preschoolers' free play—Connections with emotional and social functioning. *The International Journal of Emotional Education, 8*(1), 48–62.

Verlenden, J. V., Pampati, S., Rasberry, C., et al. (2021). Association of children's mode of school instruction with child and parent experiences and well-being during the COVID-19 Pandemic, COVID Experiences Survey, United States, October 8–November 13, 2020. *MMWR Morb Mortal Wkly Rep 2021, 70*, 369–376. Doi: 10.15585/mmwr.mm7011a1external icon

Vygotsky, L. (1966). Play and its role in the mental development of the child. *Voprosy psikhologii, 12*, 6–18.

Waite, R., & Ryan, R. (2020). *Adverse childhood experiences: What students and health professionals need to know.* Routledge.

White, J., Flynt, M., & Draper, K. (1997). Kinder therapy: Teachers as therapeutic agents. *International Journal of Play Therapy, 6*(2), 33–49. Doi: 10.1037/h0089407

White, J., Flynt, M., & Jones, N. P. (1999). Kinder therapy: An Adlerian approach for training teachers to be therapeutic agents through play. *The Journal of Individual Psychology, 55*(3), 365–382.

Wilson, B., & Ray, D. (2018). Child centered play therapy: Aggression, empathy, and self-regulation. *Journal of Counseling & Development, 96*, 399–409.

Zee, M., & Roorda, D. L. (2018). Student–teacher relationships in elementary school: The unique role of shyness, anxiety, and emotional problems. *Learning & Individual Differences, 67*, 156–166. Doi: 10.1016/j.lindif.2018.08.006

Zeng, S., Corr, C. P., O'Grady, C., & Guan, Y. (2019). Adverse childhood experiences and preschool suspension expulsion: A population study. *Child Abuse & Neglect, 97*, 104149. Doi: 10.1016/j.chiabu.2019.104149

Index

Note: **Bold** page numbers refer to tables; *italic* page numbers refer to figures.

For Product Safety Concerns and Information please contact our EU
representative GPSR@taylorandfrancis.com
Taylor & Francis Verlag GmbH, Kaufingerstraße 24, 80331 München, Germany

www.ingramcontent.com/pod-product-compliance
Ingram Content Group UK Ltd.
Pitfield, Milton Keynes, MK11 3LW, UK
UKHW031041080625
459435UK00013B/570